THE
FEEL-GOOD
HIT
A memoir
OF THE
YEAR

THE FEEL-GOOD

HIT

A memoir

OF THE YEAR

Liam Pieper

HAMISH HAMILTON
an imprint of
PENGUIN BOOKS

HAMISH HAMILTON

Published by the Penguin Group
Penguin Group (Australia)
707 Collins Street, Melbourne, Victoria 3008, Australia
(a division of Penguin Australia Pty Ltd)
Penguin Group (USA) Inc.
375 Hudson Street, New York, New York 10014, USA
Penguin Group (Canada)
90 Eglinton Avenue East, Suite 700, Toronto, Canada ON M4P 2Y3
(a division of Penguin Canada Books Inc.)
Penguin Books Ltd
80 Strand, London WC2R 0RL England
Penguin Ireland
25 St Stephen's Green, Dublin 2, Ireland
(a division of Penguin Books Ltd)
Penguin Books India Pvt Ltd
11 Community Centre, Panchsheel Park, New Delhi – 110 017, India
Penguin Group (NZ)
67 Apollo Drive, Rosedale, Auckland 0632, New Zealand
(a division of Penguin New Zealand Pty Ltd)
Penguin Books (South Africa) (Pty) Ltd
Rosebank Office Park, Block D, 181 Jan Smuts Avenue, Parktown North, Johannesburg, 2196, South Africa
Penguin (Beijing) Ltd
7F, Tower B, Jiaming Center, 27 East Third Ring Road North, Chaoyang District, Beijing 100020, China

Penguin Books Ltd, Registered Offices: 80 Strand, London WC2R 0RL, England

First published by Penguin Group (Australia), 2014

1 3 5 7 9 10 8 6 4 2

Text copyright © Liam Pieper 2014

The moral right of the author has been asserted

The following is a true story, mostly. For brevity or clarity, the chronologies of some incidents have
been condensed or altered, while some names and character details have been changed to protect identities
and organisations. With these exceptions, the events depicted in this book are true to the best of
the author's recollection, although, frankly, his memory isn't what it used to be. And the author's father
would like to assert that he does not smoke nearly as much pot as is depicted.

Design by John Canty © Penguin Group (Australia)
Cover photograph by S. Pieper
Author photograph © Tara Nielsen
Typeset in Adobe Caslon Pro
Printed and bound in Australia by Griffin Press, an accredited ISO AS/NZS 14001
Environmental Management Systems printer

National Library of Australia Cataloguing-in-Publication data:

Pieper, Liam, author.
The feel-good hit of the year / Liam Pieper.
9780670077557 (paperback)
Pieper, Liam. Authors, Australian–Biography. Drug dealers–Australia–Biography.
Drug abuse–Australia. Youth–Drug use–Australia. Popular culture–Australia.

362.2930994

penguin.com.au

FOR ARDIAN

CONTENTS

They speak of my drinking,
but never think of my thirst.

— SCOTTISH PROVERB

UP, UP AND AWAY

I

I was born on stage. To be precise, a stage in the music room of Labassa, a derelict manor house in Melbourne's south-eastern suburbs. I was born by the bay windows, where beams of light punched through the stained glass to make a century's worth of dust dance. My parents had decided I would be delivered there because the stage had the best light in the dim room, which had been designed for concerts, not childbirth, and my dad needed all the help he could get.

My parents had engaged the services of a midwife, a member of my mother's feminist collective, but she hadn't turned up. They had called her when Mum went into labour, waking her. After promising to call a doctor and come around soon, the midwife passed out again, leaving my young parents holding the ball. Mine was to be a home-birth, because, according to Dad, he and Mum wanted my 'welcome into the world to be done in a gentle and loving manner'.

In practice, when Mum started pushing with no midwife handy, my parents did what any inexperienced hippies would have and freaked out. My mum screamed and clutched at Dad, who was doing his best under the circumstances. Dad didn't know how to deliver a baby: this was 1984, he couldn't google it. He'd seen it done once before, five years earlier, when my brother Ardian had been born in the room next door, delivered with stern efficiency by the preferred doctor of Mum's collective. Dad was a quick study, though, and safely brought me, squalling, into the gentle and loving world.

Labassa is a sprawling 35-room manor that was remodelled in 1890 by Alexander Robertson, one of the transport magnates behind Cobb & Co., who sunk his fortune into property. It was built as a family home, and, more than that, to show off Robertson's unbelievable wealth. In the centre of 15 acres of parkland, Labassa was all ostentation: ballrooms, grand halls, parquetry and marble statuary. It was magnificent – the ultimate in nineteenth-century flamboyance, from the embossed wallpaper to a three-storey tower that loomed over the manor and its grounds. Later the parkland was sold off for housing and the manor itself was crudely subdivided with fibro and wood into flats, and then gradually declined into something a little more slum-ish.

By the time I was born, Labassa was a palimpsest of the lives herded through there by the fickle twentieth century. The walls of the grand entrance hall and front rooms were stained with cigar smoke from the twenties. In the forties it was bought by an émigré business-man, a Polish Jew who'd fled Nazi persecution, and it went through a string of Jewish owners who sponsored refugee families. In the fifties it housed many Jewish survivors of the Holocaust, who pieced their lives back together as best they could, kosher-butchering their poultry in the upstairs bathroom, where two decades later hippies would take acid and lie back to relax as the Victorian murals turned into Magic Eye puzzles. A wave of drug-addled beatniks then moved in, and throughout the sixties and seventies the place was frequently raided by the cops, until the beatniks were finally driven out and replaced by a group of more restrained, cerebral bohemians, including my family, and then, in 1984, me.

Mum had moved into flat 2 in 1976, taking over the lease from her older sister and brother-in-law, who'd had enough of hippies for one lifetime and shifted to the country to build a farmhouse out of mudbricks. Dad met her two years later and within three months he'd moved in too. They paid $17 a week for a pretty majestic piece of real estate.

Our flat comprised four rooms: the music room, designed for chamber orchestras, with its finely tuned acoustics that bounced sound off high ceilings and mahogany pillars; a billiard room, with chandeliers and gold-filigree wallpaper; a cramped annex retrofitted with a tiny kitchen and bathroom; and a dirty white smoking room that my folks called 'the Winter Palace', as it was the only room in the place you could successfully heat. We lived nomadically within the flat – we'd move from room to room, depending on the season, to make the most of the heat that leached out through the big bay windows.

It always seemed to be next to freezing. If you were in the flat for more than a few hours, the chill crept under your corduroy trousers and cable-knit jumper, wrapped itself around your bones and drew out your warmth until you rang cold and hollow. Everyone who lived there was sick eight months out of the year. I would sleep in the music room, with the fire burning, but in the night mist would seep in through the windows. By morning a thick fog hung near the ceiling, veiling the frescoes and sending tendrils creeping down the walls to the floor.

Apart from my family, most other residents were young artists and tradies, often both, but a long way off from starting families. There were only a couple of small children in the house during the eighties, apart from my brother and myself, but the place was always lousy with them – visitors often brought their kids around to play in the gardens or race up and down the grand staircase. As an adult I listen to friends from more privileged backgrounds talk blithely about their childhood visits to Paris and New York and think, *I hate you, you gilded cunt*, until I remember that I was raised in the fog-bound ruins of a gothic castle.

When I tell people I grew up in a house full of hippies, their first, slightly offensive question is whether my dad is really my dad. They were bohemian, sure, but it wasn't a sixties-style commune with everybody jumping in and out of each other's futons. They were all a bit too square for that. My parents got together in Australia in the late seventies: the White Australia policy had ended only a few years before, whaling was still an industry, Prime Minister Malcolm Fraser was carefully dismantling the public sector, and unemployment levels were soaring. Melbourne might have missed out on a San Francisco–style summer of love, but it was about ready for the world's biggest scummy share house.

At a basic level, Labassa was a place where people who cared about music, art and culture could live and pursue those things for not much money. It was kind of an artists' colony for broke snobs – a refuge in a beige suburban desert. Over the years a menagerie of students, artists, writers and musicians had moved in, hung around for a while, drunk wine and pretended to be Oscar Wilde, then hooked up, shacked up and moved out, to be replaced by younger models.

Mum was part of a separatist feminist collective that ran a safe space for battered women. This was before the term 'safe space' had been co-opted by terrible poetry circles, back when it meant a place where at-risk women could go without being, you know, murdered. As the location had to be kept secret, the collective used to come together for outreach meetings in places on neutral ground – such as our flat. When they came around Dad had to make himself scarce, lurking in the music room like a pallid, vegetarian phantom.

I slept in a cot by my parents' bed, and whenever there was a special occasion, a party or concert or reading, they would push all our possessions into a corner and let the hippies through. It made sense, I suppose – the room's stage and acoustics lent themselves to performance. The trickle of money that events like that brought in helped as well. They were always broke.

Mum and Dad worked odd jobs in factories and shops, bringing in just enough cash to pursue what they really cared about – he studied literature during the day and wrote plays at night, while Mum painted and practised yoga in front of the TV. To make ends meet, they would sublet part of our flat to those passing through. An artist called Jack Cash lived in the Winter Palace for a while. He was talented, charming and eccentric, but over time his behaviour became stranger and stranger. He started bringing home roadkill so he could study the anatomy to further his sketching. When he decided to keep a dead cat in the fridge, my folks had a conundrum. On the one hand they were all about open-mindedness and letting your freak flag fly. On the other, they were vegetarians, and keeping a cat next to the tofu weirded them out. In the end they asked Jack to leave.

There were more than a few at Labassa who suffered from mental illness. The kind of people the place attracted – young, bright outcasts – is a population at high risk of developing psychological disorders, and some of them tipped over the edge while they were living there. Drugs were everywhere. The wisdom of the time was that weed was a harmless alternative to alcohol. Joints were passed around like Carlos Castaneda novels. People took acid to expand their minds. At least, they said that's why they did it. I've always found that hippies take acid to make other hippies interesting. This was before anyone knew that LSD and cannabis could trigger schizophrenic episodes. When people with a predisposition towards psychosis went into a trip and never came out, that was just part of the experience. If someone wanted to keep a dead cat in the fridge, that was their business.

My parents tried their hardest to ignore the expectations of the world outside the house, but those norms encroached on them. They'd had my older brother, Ardian, in 1979, and then, under pressure from their families, got married the following year. It was a simple ceremony, held in the music room, with just immediate family and a friend each backing up the bride and groom. My grandmas catered with food and flowers, and the couple exchanged vows on the stage. There was a reading from a yoga text called *Wings of Power*. Mum and Dad both wore suits, his with a sky-blue tie with a clip shaped like a guitar.

They married to make their families happy, but it only half worked. My maternal grandmother worried aloud whether a ceremony outside of a Catholic church counted as a wedding. My paternal grandfather was a little more forgiving. He picked up Ardian and held him, saying, 'I can finally hold you now because you're no longer a bastard.'

Mum's sister – my eldest aunt – stared daggers at my dad throughout the ceremony because a week earlier her husband's brother had warned him that Dad was a junkie and begged her not to let him into the family. Dad wasn't a junkie – indeed, he'd never even seen smack – but he did love his weed, and he looked like Easy Rider dressed as John Lennon for Halloween.

The ceremony had its detractors inside the house as well. Love was precious, sure, but marriage was awfully conformist, bourgeois even. People were starting to whisper. By the time I was born, my parents were feeling out of place. The citizens of Labassa wanted to explore an alternative lifestyle, and while one baby was a karmic blessing, two looked like selling out.

Pressure was mounting inside Labassa and out. In 1980 the house had been put up for auction for the first time in decades, and the media took an interest. A local priest railed against the 'hippies of Labassa', denigrating the inhabitants in his sermons and the papers, which was unfair because their presence was the only thing keeping at bay the slimy property developers who were eyeing off the land, constantly creeping about in their white sandshoes, leaving business cards under the door in the night.

The long-term residents had saved the house from ruin and condemnation. People moved in for decades at a time and treated Labassa as if it were their own: tradies repaired leaky roofs and plumbing, the artists did their best to preserve the manor's murals and frescoes. In the end the National Trust bought the house, with the aim of preserving it, and slowly started squeezing out the residents. The rent went up to $32 and then $50 a week.

Around the time the Trust bought the building, a play Dad had written back in high school was getting a run with a little theatre company a few blocks over. In it, a swami (Dad had been reading a lot of *One Hand Clapping*–esque titles at the time) faces eviction from his mountain and needs to make some quick cash. He sends an envoy to the States, where he starts a cult that teaches locals how to be blissfully happy while giving up their possessions. He comes into conflict with an archetypal American villain named 'Ronald Raygun', and hilarity ensues. It's worth noting that this was all written nearly a decade before Reagan became president, so the moral of the story is that if you take enough acid, you really can see through time.

The production got some press, and an *Age* journalist came by to profile the family. Mum, Dad and Ardian were featured in a two-page spread with a series of photographs capturing the lives of the hippies in the big old mansion, and then suddenly the place was over-run with tourists.

The Trust started to hold open days, when they ushered sightseers through the grand entrance hall and ballroom. On these days we had to pack up all our shit from the front rooms of the flat and move it into the adjoining room, where we would be very quiet while the Trust led the blue-rinse set through our living room. It was like the world's most ostentatious pre-sale house inspection, where the renters have to make their lives look desirable and then disappear. While we hid in the far end of the flat, history buffs would come through and steal whatever they could – bits of woodwork, ornate tiles, scraps of wallpaper. Every time one of those open days ended we would return to find our apartment a little less grand. It was like a time-lapse video of gentrification, and it was ruining our home.

In 1986 Mum and Dad decided they needed to give us kids an opportunity to have a place to call our own, a backyard and inde-pendence from other people. They wanted to establish themselves as a family, not just tenants in a strange experiment. By then, Labassa was not a great place for kids to be. The vibe had changed. Money started going missing from wallets and from under mattresses, and Dad's bike vanished from outside the door one day. The air from the buoy-ant feeling of community was being slowly let out. The experiment may still have been magical, but it wasn't for us any more. My par-ents hung on as long as they could, but the camel's back was broken when another of the mothers in the house awoke to find a mark on her baby – a perfect imprint of a set of adult teeth. It was time to go.

2

My family moved into a two-bedroom weatherboard cottage in Oakleigh, a suburb 12 kilometres across town that at the time was the Greekest place outside of Athens. It was an area full of factory-job retirees who had moved there for the affordable houses with huge backyards, in which they drank coffee and grew grapevines for homemade retsina and yelled at my brother and me.

Suburban life was hard on my parents. Deep down they hadn't wanted to leave Labassa and so they had trouble adjusting to life outside it. Even now they miss their old life of bohemian fuck-aroundery. They never really got over it in the long run, and in the short term things got very hard, very quickly.

Having first balanced the books and worked out that they could just manage payments on the Oakleigh house, my parents bought it. Not long after they signed the papers, the recession hit and interest rates shot up to 17.5 per cent, leaving them with a mortgage they could barely service. With no pool of hippies to look after the kids and no money to hire babysitters, Mum and Dad's world shrunk. There were no more poetry readings or plays or feminist collectives or long nights spent smoking weed and jamming to Paul Simon. Where there was once experimental art and philosophical exploration, there were now dirty laundry and meals for fussy children and utility disconnection notices.

Mum was working at a family planning clinic and Dad was stacking shelves at a supermarket by night while struggling to finish his arts degree at Monash University by day. Then Mum fell pregnant with my little brother Hamish, and we were, for the foreseeable future, fucked.

Since we had no money, Mum used to bring home odds and ends for us to play with from a hospital she pulled cleaning shifts at sometimes. There were bandages for when we wanted to be Egyptian mummies and huge spinal-tap syringes that we used as water guns, which was neat since we weren't allowed to play with toy guns, because of Vietnam. One of my favourite playthings was a promotional paperweight from the clinic, a packet of birth-control pills encased in resin, which I would prop up below the TV and pretend was the control panel for a starship. We made our own fun.

Ardian used to roam the streets collecting aluminium cans, for which a local recycling centre would pay him one cent apiece. He'd carry them in a huge hessian sack that he dragged behind him like a Dickensian-era Pooh Bear. Charismatic and inventive, even as a pre-teen, he petitioned neighbourhood bars and alcoholics to store up their empties and hand them over to him in bulk. Once he'd collected several thousand cans, he cashed them in and bought an Atari, then passed the gig on to me.

Endless bills, no sleep and less money took their toll. After Hamish was born in 1989, Mum sank into postnatal depression, which in turn sent Dad into a funk. When I think back to my early childhood, there were a lot of dark Roald Dahl novels and art-house movies, a lot of time spent listening to classical guitar or walking along wintry, windswept beaches. The whole family had a melancholic streak.

Dad had it the worst. He was wise but had been blasted by life, just like Gandalf the White in the stories he would read me at bedtime. Sometimes he'd take us fishing, which was always a special time for my brothers and me, each of us throwing a line into the water and staring moodily out over the waves. He encouraged me to express myself through music. I would rush home from piano lessons on the weekend to play heart-rending, *con dolore* renditions of 'The Entertainer' and the *Pink Panther* theme song.

Before I could even really comprehend the world, I had inherited his world view. I was a sad, thoughtful kid. Dad taught me to appreciate the transient beauty in life. One time a butterfly landed on his hand and he held it out to show me the patterns on its wings. 'Look how beautiful it is. Look at the colours, their majesty. It will only live for a few hours,' he told me. 'A few hours of flight, of magnificence, after a lifetime of crawling on its belly.'

My parents never fought while they lived at Labassa. Now it was all they did. They fought about money, about each other, about school fees and clothing and food and us. In fits of rage they would scream and wail, punch holes in walls, threaten each other, threaten to leave.

Mum and Dad called each other names. They blamed each other for ruining their lives. They blamed us kids for ruining their lives. We siblings responded in different ways. When they fought, I would rush to the piano and bang out an up-tempo 'Moonlight Sonata', thinking they might be dazzled by my unique interpretation of Beethoven and stop arguing to come in and applaud me.

Hamish had it figured out the best, despite being all of four. He would wait until the raised voices reached their crescendo before running full bore into the kitchen table, smacking his forehead against the wood. From my piano stool I would hear a terrifying crack, then a moment of shocked silence before Hamish started wailing, and Mum and Dad scrambled to comfort him. Full marks, little brother.

Ardian was more resilient. He was older, tougher; he had an undercut. One time my mother came into the lounge room where we were watching TV, yelling, 'Your father and I are getting divorced. Are you happy now?' Ardian just fixed her with a withering look from under his fringe. 'Yes, Mum. I'm very happy. That was the plan all along.' Or he would flick his hair out of his eyes and sneer, 'Why don't you just have a fucking joint and calm down?' This was actually the best thing for it. After a day of screaming histrionics, my parents would roll a joint and start cuddling on the couch.

Having been ingloriously stranded in the suburbs, my parents hung on to the time they could spend stoned as a link to the old world. Pot smoke was our matzo ball soup. After work, on the weekend, whenever friends came around, they would roll pinched single-paper joints, made with Tally-Ho papers, Drum tobacco and sticky home-grown. 'Numbers', they called them, as in, 'Let's have a number,' or 'Roll me a number, honey,' as in, Number One, Two, Three, Four.

Dad refused to believe that marijuana could be anything other than a treasure of Olympus, brought to him at Promethean cost, and he thought it should be treated with according respect. Specifically, he would not be shaken from his conviction that weed was ambrosia for creative minds and sent the muse bouncing like a gummy bear. He scoffed at the idea that weed hindered artistic ambitions, or any ambition, for that matter. To him it was inconceivable that smoking weed every day could be a bad thing.

'Everyone knows that weed makes you more creative,' he would say, opening a bag of Doritos. 'It's been proven by science.'

Dad was widely read, and had an encyclopaedic knowledge of art spanning highbrow and low: he could tell you anything you needed to know about French existentialism or Britpop or the links between them. When I was small, he'd help me brush my teeth and get into my pyjamas, then play me a song on the guitar, which would lead to a discursive monologue: what I ought to know about the history of bluegrass, steel string and Steely Dan, how Steely Dan was named after a steam-powered dildo in a William Burroughs book, whether I wanted him to read me some Burroughs, and did I know what a dildo was?

He'd at last completed his degree with honours, which rendered him both unemployable and capable of wielding critical theory to cut down dissenters or dismantle any arguments that ran contrary to his lifestyle. The latter is a trick many Australian baby boomers mastered: they'd had free education and weren't afraid to use it. The seventies had been a perfect storm of apologist philosophies used to justify terrible behaviour. If you could think of a buzzword like 'sex addiction' or 'workaholism', you could get away with pretty much whatever you wanted, even decades down the track. 'I have an addictive personality,' Mum would explain, skinning up.

I should be clear: provided you are reasonably sane, I don't think smoking pot around your kids is necessarily that big a deal. At worst, it makes you kind of vague when it comes to matters of discipline. I mean, who smokes a joint and then has the energy to yell at their kids for stealing a block of chocolate? Especially since the kids have just brought home a delicious block of chocolate. In our case, Mum and Dad's fondness for pot didn't derange us – they got up every morning and worked to make us a home, and we weren't cold or neglected or in any way ill-treated as a result of their recreational drug use.

Except, perhaps, for when it came to the food, which, if what was served on our dinner table can't legally be considered child abuse, was at least morally inexcusable. It isn't fair to say my folks didn't fulfil our nutritional needs: they'd go out of their way to prepare vegetarian, karma-neutral foods. It's just that your palate has a different bent when you've had a sly toot on the old hash pipe. Mum and Dad made an effort to prepare healthy meals: squares of apple and cheese, carrot sticks, and a signature dish that was a brave Anglicisation of dhal. The recipe, picked up from the hippies, involved boiling a bag of red lentils until they liquefied, heaping the results onto bowls of microwave-cooked starchy rice, and topping the lot with White Crow tomato sauce. Dessert was often a dish we called 'butter balls'. The recipe was basic: take a spoonful of margarine and roll it in a jar of sugar until it is crusted in a half-inch of crystalline diabetes.

For a long time I didn't really understand the link between the special tobacco my folks smoked and the rhythms and quirks of life at home. I learned how to predict my parents' moods based on the time of day and how much they'd had to smoke. Dad had found work teaching at a TAFE, which brought in more money but sent him home stressed, and I knew well enough to stay scarce until he'd made a cup of coffee and had a couple of joints. If Mum plopped down at the kitchen table and called for Dad to 'roll a number, honey', that meant dinner was half an hour away, and it was a good time to lightly bring up the idea of ordering pizza. Late at night, when the light coming from my parents' room was hazy and warm, and you could hear them laughing at the television, was the perfect time to hit them up for pocket money.

I also knew that I wasn't supposed to talk about their 'green tobacco' outside the house because it could get not only me but also my parents into trouble. This was a rule I filed away alongside others that I appreciated without completely understanding, like saying please and thank you when at a friend's house, or not telling Grandma that Mum had once screamed, 'Fucking shitfuck' when she stubbed her toe.

Mum and Dad didn't subscribe to a lot of traditional child-rearing techniques. We were disciplined sporadically and with varying degrees of harshness, depending on the time of day, how much they'd had to smoke, and how worn down by the process of raising a family they were. Ardian bore the brunt of new-age parenting books, which instructed Mum and Dad to encourage him to pursue his artistic inclinations. I got less of that. While I was allowed to indulge my imagination, I was also given earnest lectures on the merits of hard work, and the occasional scolding.

By the time Hamish came along, they were like, 'Whatever. Karma will sort it out.' He was left to explore the world at his own pace, piecing together a moral code as best he could. On a daytrip to the mountains, for example, he wasn't keen on the snowshoes we'd hired and insisted on running around barefoot. He suffered frostbite but, you know, he's never run around barefoot in the snow since. The approach seemed to work out pretty well: from time to time he'd drink a bottle of white-out or something and need to be rushed to hospital, but apart from that, he did a fine job of raising himself.

My parents had done their best to raise me free of the constraints of hegemonic ideology. Instead they tried to educate me in the plurality of cultures and religions of the world, so that, if and when the time came, I would be able to choose the religion or philosophy that best suited my spiritual development.

My Catholic maternal grandmother was cool with that, but even so she had me secretly baptised one afternoon. In between visits to the zoo and the park, we ducked into the Catholic church down the road from her house, where the priest gave me a clandestine sacrament. Then she bought me ice-cream, and I completely forgot about being doused in holy water by a nice man in a gown. She did the same to my brothers, and only told my parents about it after all her grandchildren were safe from purgatory. I also picked up bits and pieces from other religions – Buddhist parables from my Malaysian godparents, scraps of Hindu and Jewish wisdom from my parents' friends – and by the time I started primary school I was a fizzing mess of confused, contradictory hippie bullshit.

On my first day of kindergarten I ruined afternoon tea by loudly lecturing Theo, an older, much bigger kid, on how he shouldn't eat the salami sandwiches his mother had made for him, because the Buddha strove towards Nirvana by abstaining from meat, and if he finished that sandwich, he was probably going to hell.

Culture shock aside, we kids learned to be happy in the suburbs. Beaten old weatherboards clad a cosy place kept warm with gun-metal heaters that we'd 'borrowed' from Labassa. My parents had one bedroom, my brothers and I the other. Hamish and I shared a bunk and Ardian slept on a fold-out bed underneath a 6-foot mural of Voltron we'd painted on the wall. At night, after we had gone to bed, Mum and Dad would have friends around for weed and instant noodles. Even now, whenever I smell the sharp chemical tang of chicken-flavoured two-minute noodles, I'm back in that overheated room in Oakleigh, listening to the ping of the bar heater cracking the darkness as my brothers snore and laughter rattles in from the living room.

A tiny whitewashed hallway separated the bedrooms from the living room and kitchen. Beyond that a slim lounge room backed onto the sunroom, a semi-detached fibro-and-glass extension. Apart from that, most of the property was backyard, but that was fine because the backyard had its charms.

In their spare time my parents tooled around the house, painting or gardening. Dad planted a feature wall of bamboo that quickly went feral and turned the yard into a great, spikey forest. Using scraps of wood and a few massive pine logs, he built us a tree house. It sat on stilts and surveyed the swaying treetops and below that a Tonka truck–filled sandpit.

We grew a lot of our own food: tomatoes and butternut pumpkins and corn, apricots and lemons, in beds neatly separated by scavenged railway sleepers. I used to help Dad in the garden, turning over shovelfuls of compost or rooting around underneath the pumpkin vines for snails, squealing if I ever touched one and getting Dad to crush it.

During the summer there were leafy, fragrant plants in a corner of the yard that was cut off from prying eyes by a ring of bamboo. They smelled wonderful and had a ticklish texture. They were about as tall as I was, and on hot days I liked to crawl underneath them and watch the sunlight through the serrated leaves. If I lay on my back and reached up, I could just touch the foliage and let the leaves brush my fingertips.

Towards autumn Mum and Dad would uproot the plants whole and hang them upside down in the sunroom to dry. After that we weren't allowed to play near them. This didn't seem fair to me and I was forever trying to sneak into the sunroom to play among the drying racks. I complained bitterly to Dad until he explained that the plants were a special kind of tobacco that he and Mum were growing for themselves, and that I mustn't disturb them.

'Why do you have to grow it?' I whined. 'Why can't you just buy the cigarettes that are already at the milk bar?' It seemed to me that my parents wasted an inordinate amount of time rolling their fiddly little roaches. It seemed much smarter to go for store-bought darts, like the Holiday menthols that one gravel-voiced friend of Mum's smoked when she came around.

'We can't afford to,' Dad explained, truthfully. 'And even if we could, this is very special tobacco.'

'Why?'

'Well . . . it helps grown-ups relax.'

'Can I try it?'

'No. Not until you're older.'

Back then all that special green tobacco would last the family the year. Once it was dry my parents packed it up and stored it, and I'd quickly forget my fascination with the forbidden sunroom of mystery and move on to other pursuits, such as trying to convince the kid next door to lend me his Nintendo. The crop didn't really register beyond my seeing it as a seasonal chore. The house wasn't full of junkies or bong smoke; drug dealers never came knocking. Like millions of Australians, Mum and Dad just liked to unwind by passing around a spliff and giggling into a cheese toastie. The worst that could be said about them was that they were paranoid about the neighbourhood.

In the early nineties, Oakleigh, though sleepy during the day, could be sketchy come night-time. My folks worried about local gangs that were growing in power and influence – or, at least, that were tagging buildings closer and closer to our house. Ardian, who was just about to graduate from primary school, would come back from class telling horror stories about the Oakleigh Wogs.

The Wogs were a gang that had been around Oakleigh for a couple of decades before we moved there. They were scary as fuck and great marketers. According to urban legend they'd started as a soccer team. Not long after the huge wave of Aegean immigration following World War Two flooded Melbourne's east side, those Greek families had first-generation Australian children who banded together after being victimised by the Anglo kids in the area. The team formed a bond that transcended the soccer field and eventually they started to stand up for themselves against the skippies. As the gang grew in numbers, the original members moved into low-rent extortion and drug peddling. In time the older generation groomed the new into becoming semi-professional criminals.

Everyone knew someone who'd been robbed or beaten or stabbed by a Wog. Their tag, a 'W' spray-painted inside a circle like the anarchy sign, cropped up on toilet walls, street corners and the backs of seats on the school bus.

In 1992, as I was entering Grade 3 and Ardian was beginning high school, a group of former students, rumoured to be tied to the Wogs, jumped the principal of my primary school in the car park, beating him with baseball bats and taking both his wallet and his car. For some reason the school chose to announce the incident at assembly. They lined us up in neat rows on the asphalt forecourt and, in between singing the national anthem and reporting on the softball championship scores, the principal described in graphic detail how he had been struck from behind, knocked to the ground and beaten to a fine paste. After his attackers fled with his money and transport, he crawled across the playground and up the steps towards the school. By the time he reached the large double doors, his hands were too slippery with blood to work the doorknob, so he collapsed and nearly bled out until he was found by another teacher.

We talked about it all day at school, exaggerating the details as we went, until that night we breathlessly told our parents about the gangland hit that had taken place in the playground. That night the school was besieged by calls from angry parents, and not long after that my folks found me another school.

Though my parents were pacifists, Dad wasn't a stranger to violence. When he and my mum first met he was working as a taxi driver, a profession he gave up after he drove a couple of guys to a remote street near the Tullamarine Freeway, where they brained him with a brick and stole his change belt. They caught the fuckers eventually, and Dad's testimony put one of them behind bars, where he was later beaten to death. The other guy disappeared but they found him in the end, dismembered with a hacksaw and sealed in a barrel that had sunk to the bottom of the Yarra.

So my folks were rationalists, if not realists, and when the threat of violence in Oakleigh got a little too real, we upped stakes and moved a couple of suburbs over, where the local public high school had a reputation for getting public-school kids into good universities, the streets were clean and quiet, and people were happy to mind their own business. The neighbours were all reclusive grandmas and ambitious boomer families. Nobody bothered anyone else, and nobody knew what a dope plant looked like.

3

We acclimatised soon enough and mostly enjoyed a nice, wholesome suburban existence. There were moments when the veneer cracked, though, and the undercurrent of benign lawlessness welled up, such as the time Mum and Dad threw a dinner party.

Some workmates of Dad's had come over and I'd been told to go outside and play. I was being Wolverine, crawling on my belly across the backyard and clumsily trying to pop my claws, which I'd fashioned out of satay sticks and a pair of mittens, when I noticed an odd sound coming from our shed.

The shed was always secured, a fact I simply took for granted, which was strange because I was the type of child obsessed by any kind of locked door. Ordinarily the idea that something was being kept from me would have lodged in my brain like a tick, eating away at me until I was nothing but a keening mess, scratching at the door until my fingers were bloody stumps. However, I'd been in the shed when we first moved in, and I knew there was nothing in there but dust and old paint tins. Now, though, there was this weird noise coming from inside.

I pressed my ear to the door. There it was: a low, crackling hum. Maybe a nest of wasps had made its home in there? I dropped to my knees and peeked under the door, then recoiled with a little shriek. Something was lighting up the room, creating a dull glow even in the daylight. I thought hard for a moment and then scrambled inside.

Mum and Dad had finished dinner and were standing around the living room with their friends, admiring one of Mum's paintings. I ran up and tugged at Dad's sleeve. 'Dad! There's something in the shed.'

Mum and Dad shot each other an alarmed look and then smiled uneasily. Dad did that thing where you muss a kid's hair affectionately and move your palm across their face to manouevre them behind you. He smiled politely at his guests. 'Nothing wrong with your imagination, is there, kiddo?'

I squirmed out of his grasp, indignant. 'I'm not imagining things! There's something in the shed and it glows white and it sounds like bees and you have to come to look now!' Dad's face darkened as he pulled me into a tight hug against his hip, muzzling me with a hand.

'Too much imagination maybe!' he said, laughing awkwardly, and everyone else joined in.

I tried Ardian, who was in his room, cleaning his gun. Back then he carried a hydraulic replica Beretta that fired little plastic pellets hard enough to penetrate walls, and I lived in terror of it. If I bothered him or burst into his room while he was with his girlfriend, he would wave it at me threateningly. While I wasn't sure that kind of firepower offered any protection against whatever was out there, it couldn't hurt to go in armed. I told him there was something in the shed, including the details of the strange light and the buzzing noise.

'I think it's a ghost!' I whispered.

'Of course it's a ghost,' he chirped. 'It's the ghost of the old man who was murdered in your room before we moved in. That's why we got the house so cheap, and that's why we aren't allowed to open the shed door. The ghost is trapped in there for now but if we let it out, it will skin us all while we sleep.'

To prove his point, he sneaked me out of bed that night and we commando-crawled past the adults watching TV in the lounge and out to the shed. He motioned for me to scuttle up to the door and peer into the crack beneath it, from which the otherworldly glow seeped.

I didn't sleep that night. Or for quite a while after. Instead I would lie awake and shiver, convinced that if I closed my eyes the ghost would get me. Throughout that winter, as the sleepless nights added up, I campaigned for my folks to do something about the haunting, only to be rebuffed. I couldn't understand how they could be so blasé about the *evil undead spirit* living in our shed, the supernatural but nonetheless clear-and-present danger. I tried to explain this to Mum and Dad night after night, but they just wearily told me to go back to bed. They broke eventually and at the end of that season they dismantled the hydroponic rig they'd been running in the shed and started growing their crops out in the open. Given that our neighbours were almost exclusively elderly Greeks who only ventured outside to water their concrete, my parents figured we'd be safe.

They didn't count on Francois, the fifteen-year-old kid from across the road who, about a year after we moved in, kicked his footy into our yard and jumped over the fence to retrieve it, to find himself standing in our pot crop. He came back later that night to steal a couple of plants, which wouldn't have been a big deal if he'd been a little smarter about it.

I can't remember Francois that well, so I won't impugn his character by stating that he was a fucking idiot, but I will say he came from a region in rural France infamous for its inbreeding. There were fifteen or so plants in our backyard. He stole two and stripped them in the backyard of the old lady who lived behind our place. Thinking someone was vandalising her garden, she called the cops, who peeked over the fence and noticed the dozen-odd weed plants dotting our backyard.

Meanwhile, Francois had been caught trying to sell our pot in the playground. When the school handed him over to the police, he told the cops that my folks had sold him the weed, and that they had much, much more. The grass he'd stolen was immature, uncured,

unsaleable: no self-respecting dealer in the world would have ped-
dled it, not even to someone like Francois, whose intellectual faculties
were blunted by a storm of defective genes from generations of furtive
incest, probably. His story was clearly horseshit, but it was enough to
secure a warrant to raid our house the next morning.

Dad was feeding the cat when they arrested him. Ulysses was a sweet,
stupid animal and all he wanted from life was to eat. From the second
he got up to the moment when he fell asleep, he would stand in the
kitchen mewing with the polite, steady rhythm of a gondolier's cry.
My dad, a light sleeper, was usually the first up, and he was shaking
out the contents of a Whiskas box into a tray when he looked up to
see a detective holding a weapon on him.

Ulysses dashed away as the plainclothes officers tackled and
cuffed Dad, returning a moment later to dine after surmising that the
Armoured Regional Response Team swarming through the house
was not interested in his breakfast.

When it comes to raids, there are two kinds of cops: the old and
sensibly jaded, and the young and dangerous. Every raiding unit has a
few surly youths who find it just as unbelievable as I do that someone
has armed them, and they charge into the situation like extras from
a crime drama, all fired up on the adrenaline of kicking down a door.

These cops were the excitable kind, running on the intelligence
they'd extracted from Francois that painted my folks as drug lords. So,
as the response team dashed through the house, they were dismayed

to find it full of children. They stomped about for a while, crunching Lego underfoot and tripping over stuffed toys in their search for contraband, until they realised they weren't going to find a secret meth lab on the premises.

You could tell they weren't sure how to interact with us kids. We were too young to push around and our tiny wrists couldn't hold bracelets. After a while they just ignored us and went about their business, turning the house upside down while we howled for Weet-Bix and for someone to turn on the cartoons.

In the end, a kindly older cop took us outside and let us ride in his patrol car while my parents were being rounded up.

'Can I play with the siren?' I asked.

'You're not supposed to sound the siren unless there's an emergency.'

'Isn't this an emergency?'

'Oh, go on then.'

Weeeeeeeeeeee!

He leaned over and switched it off. Outside my dad was being put in the back of a paddy wagon. I turned to the cop and implored, 'Please? Just one more?'

Weeeeeeeeeeee!

What fun! It was like being inside the *Ghostbusters* car, and I imagine that doing the same thing today would be as wicked fun as it was then.

My uncle was summoned to look after us while Mum and Dad went down to the station for processing. The cops were decent enough about it. The only brutality my parents endured was from one disappointed senior sergeant who clucked his tongue, shook his head and gently berated them: 'Come on, guys! You're too old for this shit.'

After Mum and Dad had been dragged outside in their pyjamas and arrested in front of the flashing lights, the neighbours turned frosty. People jogging by and those collecting the morning paper had stood and gawked. It had never been the kind of neighbourhood where we used to pop over to each other's houses to borrow sugar, and after the arrest many in our street ended up perfecting the constipated half-smile and quick look-away whenever they encountered us. When both my parents and the family across the street were in the front garden of a Sunday, they would studiously ignore each other, pruning their rose bushes with immaculate concentration.

A few months afterwards my parents went to court and emerged with a conviction for possessing and cultivating a drug of dependence. This wasn't ideal, but we consoled ourselves with the knowledge that things could have been much worse. Things would get worse, as it turns out, but not for a while, and until then we had other things to worry about. We had school in the morning, for one thing, at a campus where all the teachers now thought my folks were drug dealers.

4

After the arrest, Ardian got a hard time from his teachers, who had decided he was a bad seed. Hamish and I were still in primary school, he was just starting, I was about to leave, but Ardian was in the middle of high school. His school, while state-run, regularly turned out graduating classes with grades consistent with those of private schools, which meant an awful lot to families of limited means. They achieved this, year after year, through judicious Darwinism, by expelling troublesome students before they could affect the median grade of graduating classes.

It's not that the teachers themselves were particularly inspiring.

There were a few good ones but the faculty was largely a gallery of alcoholics and aspiring novelists who had washed up teaching high school after their other dreams didn't pan out. Chief among these was Ms B, who had a fling with Ardian and tried to get him to elope to Sydney days before his final exams. He called us in the morning from the airport and casually mentioned that he was going to skip town with his English teacher.

'There's nothing weird about it. We're going to get a hotel and visit John Marsden!' My dad thought that wasn't a great idea, and drove up to the airport to drag him back home.

My parents complained to the school, but, whatever discipline they handed down, she kept her job, she kept on fucking her students, and, when I was old enough to be in her class, she went on to take it out on me. She had a hard time demarcating between my older, Jeff Buckley–esque brother, and me. Years after their affair ended, for the semester I had her for English, she would often give me detention, then wait until we were alone and tearfully ask me why I continued to neglect my homework 'after all we've been through together'. I still see her sometimes when I head out to the suburbs to visit family, standing in line at the supermarket, or shoplifting from the chemist.

Ardian was five years older than me, and he had the perfect combination of good looks, intelligence and utter lack of ambition that makes kids nightmarish students. He spent his time fighting, smoking and chasing girls, and put more effort into his immaculate undercut than his studies, but still managed to get decent grades. The formative part of Ardian's youth had been spent in the bohemian era of our family, and he wore that influence pretty heavily. He played music: grunge guitar before Kurt's shotgun, jazz piano after. He'd been a ladies' man long before he was old enough to drive, and he was always pulling off outrageous stunts. When his girlfriend had to go to school on her birthday, he went out the night before to spray-paint a billboard that her bus passed by with 'Ardian ♥s Callie'.

Rumours were always circulating about him, about the way he romanced his girlfriends by taking them hitchhiking up to Sydney, where they'd break into expensive hotels to use their spas, mini-bars and beds. At our high school, which had all the soul of the town from *Footloose*, he was legendary, for his free spirit, for his fondness for women. To this day I can be drinking in a bar anywhere on the east coast and some beautiful stranger will come up to me to tell me that she knew my brother.

He was particularly keen on hallucinogens. These were objects of sweet nostalgia for my parents from their Labassa days, which they encouraged Ardian to take instead of going out drinking and getting into fights. When he and his friends had gone mushrooming in the countryside or scored some LSD, they would take it and hang out in the lounge room, while Mum bustled in and out with sandwiches and glasses of cordial, and my dad put on a Cat Stevens video and held court about how he'd done acid once but 'it never really did anything for me'.

I looked forward to the times when Ardian would return from some hippie festival devoted to nudity and djembe drumming to drop the last of his LSD in the house. He would coax a couple of teenaged girls back home with him and they would sit on the roof, watching the clouds and taking photos of each other's feet. Mum took this in her stride, as though it was the most natural thing in the world. Whenever one of the girls would stumble inside to show Mum a Polaroid of her ankle or whatever, Mum just smiled encouragingly and made her some fairy bread.

Years later, when I would come home strung out after staying up for days on pills and coke, wide-eyed and gibbering, Mum would knock on my bedroom door to ask if something was the matter. 'I'm okay, Mum!' I would yell. 'I've just taken some bad acid!' Mum would have been mortified to know that I'd been dabbling with powders – she has a trenchant distrust of all drugs besides pot and hallucinogens – but she knew what to do with a bad acid trip, and would prop me up on the couch with a cup of tea and a *Star Trek* video.

I adored Ardian and emulated him in everything he did, taking pains to model my speech and vocabulary after his. The jumpers and jeans I received as hand-me-downs were treasures, and I wore them until they were hanging off me in strips of tie-dye and corduroy. When he had girls over I would hang around in the lounge room, surreptitiously flexing my muscles, or rushing to the piano to play Doors covers to try to get them to notice me. I adopted my family's counter-cultural rebellion and artistic leanings early on, or at least my interpretation of them: I was sure that if I could just smoke dope I would somehow absorb some of that cool.

In the evenings Ardian would have friends over to sit around a camp-
fire in the backyard, punch cones and talk nonsense. Normally Ardian
got a bit shitty if I tried to hang out with his friends, but when they
were baked they seemed to enjoy my company. I savoured those occasions, talking to the older boys about grown-up things like girls and
Nirvana and whether David Lynch was a genius. My jokes got laughs,
and I would flit around Ardian's mates, asking questions or trying to
scab cones. I knew from the Life Education caravan that visited my
school, with its slightly creepy giraffe puppet who warned us about
the dangers of alcohol and casual sex, that smoking cigarettes was bad
for me. But the impression I got from my family was that marijuana
was harmless, and smoking sticky hydro in a bong made from a juice
bottle seemed impossibly grown-up and glamorous.

'You're a bit young, Liam,' Ardian would grin, breathing out a
lungful of smoke and clearing the chamber by blowing on the shot-
tie. 'You have to be old enough not to want to play at the park any
more. Then you can start going to the park to get stoned.' That was a
long-running, corny joke within the family: every time I got on my
pushbike and announced that I was going to the park, my parents
would roll their eyes, nudge each other and stage whisper, 'Guess we'd
better get a burrito in the microwave for when Sir Munchenstein
over there gets home,' which would make me flush red and ride off
in a huff. I was actually going to the park to play on the roundabouts,
and it embarrassed me that I wasn't old enough to smoke yet.

The first time I got high was with my best friend Sam, who
I'd known since I was eight. Sam was the youngest brother of my

brother's best buddy and so we became friends by default. I met him when the whole family came over for a play date. The adults pulled out joints and beers and guitars and set up in the lounge room, while Ardian and his friends went off to smoke in the backyard. To shake me from tailing him all day, Ardian introduced me to Sam, who was milling about shyly out the front of the house. He was kind of sporty, a jock kid, but we bonded over a shared love of throwing rocks at cars and then running like hell.

We were about twelve when, on a sleepover, we stole some of Ardian's weed and rolled it into a clumsy joint. Together, Sam and I stuck our eager little faces out of the bedroom window and passed the blunt back and forth, watching as the smoke billowed out into the night and the universe opened up for us. Suddenly we understood all those foreign, esoteric, grown-up things that until now we'd only pretended to like: art-house movies, anime, jam bands, endless guitar solos. Getting high was like finding a pamphlet that explained how to get the most out of our leisure time, and that was all we did for the next couple of years. Weed around my way was exceptionally strong: a demonic ultra-grass bred over decades of sinister experimentation in hydro labs. It was potent, sticky gear, covered in tiny brown hairs that glistened with psychedelic menace. Unscrupulous drug dealers who sold inferior hydro used to spray their crops with Pepsi to mimic the texture.

I was shy, and filling my head with anaesthetic-strength cannabinoids didn't help. While other kids our age were playing sport and going to films and fingering each other, Sam and I stayed in his room and watched videos. It turns out that weed isn't glamorous, but that's the problem with getting stoned all the time: you forget how to be bored and start enjoying things like Pink Floyd films and Australian hip-hop. Looking back at it now, I'm surprised no one told us to go outside and play. Actually, Mum did once, after she'd busted me hiding a bag of pot in my bedroom.

'What's this?'

'Um . . .'

'Are you smoking pot now?'

'Ummm . . . Yes?'

'Right . . . Well, be careful. And remember that some people are going to judge you for smoking pot, and not want to be your friend. And don't forget to keep friends around that don't smoke. And don't smoke it before bed because it'll keep you up thinking about bullshit. And do your homework. And never fucking touch my stash, okay?'

It was good advice but it came far too late. By the time I started high school, I was already a wan, shiftless burnout, suspicious of authority and unconvinced that school could teach me anything I hadn't learned from hanging out with older kids. On my first day of Year 7, the vice principal collared me in the hallway and examined my face.

'Ah, shit,' he lamented. 'Another Pieper.'

PEAKING
AT
HIGH SCHOOL

5

I was a very strange little teenager, and smoking weed didn't help. I liked girls and rock and roll and Pokemon, and I had no idea where to draw the lines between them. Sam had gone to another high school and I was a cripplingly shy kid, the kind who spent lunchtimes plodding lonely circles of the oval. I would have liked to play Dungeons & Dragons but couldn't find anyone who was into it. This was pre-internet, before people could easily meet like-minded weirdos and get their kinks seen to.

My words came out in choked-off half sentences that made no sense, even to me. These stillborn communiqués broke across the faces of people I tried to talk to in waves: confusion, incomprehension, dismissal. I was a nice enough guy but my nerves made me creepy, clumsy – forever stumbling about, mumbling nonsense. The first time I heard Radiohead's 'Creep' it was so cathartic it broke me open and scraped me out like I was some angst-ridden lobster. Of course, back then I wasn't hip to Radiohead; I was just a creep.

I had no idea how to talk to people, even other misfit lads, let alone girls. I used to hang around at parties and then take over the piano to sing one of my ballads, which were just plagiarised Leonard Cohen songs with the names and location references switched up.

In the first week of high school I developed a crush on a classmate, Lilly, which was as spectacularly profound as it was unrequited. I would spend close to a decade trying to woo her, and fail. She wanted nothing to do with me, and she had her reasons.

Throughout the early years of high school, when not in uniform, I wore the same thing every day: a black denim jacket over a white T-shirt with black tracksuit pants. It was shapeless and baggy, which I thought hid the fact that I was as well. Short and dumpy, I could arrange the folds of denim and polyester to preclude any hint as to what my body might look like. At thirteen I imagined the ensemble to be quite stylish, like a relaxed tuxedo – something James Bond might slip into in a post-coital languor while he searched for his cigarettes – but were someone to wear that same outfit on school premises past the age of consent, they would end up on a government watch list pretty sharpish. My skin was fighting a losing battle against grotesque, infected pimples that would pop up and refuse to leave until

I squeezed them into scars. I wore my hair in a long, greasy ponytail, and I can't imagine I smelt very nice. In short, I was a catch.

I passed my lunchtimes reading or hanging out with the twitchy outcasts who had annexed the foursquare court and swapped tips on hacking PlayStations and bomb making. Now and then I got detention, which I enjoyed because it gave me an excuse to read for an hour without having to talk to anyone.

Then, one day during my fourteenth year, things changed. A group of kids I vaguely knew invited me to smoke weed with them. They were musicians. Not the fun kind, mind. Not the kind with cool haircuts and guitars and smack habits and girlfriends; these were jazz musicians. It was still better, though, than hanging around with the kids at school who spoke Elvish. The jazz musicians asked if I knew where they could score some grass. I told them I'd be happy to help.

There was always weed around the house, down the back of the couch, spilling out of an open baggie on the kitchen table or stowed away in my parents' filing cabinet, the lock of which I could pick with a pen lid. I stole a chunk and went to hang out with my new buddies, Ben, Marco and Jules, determined to buy their friendship with it.

Ben's dad was away on business and we stood in his backyard, rolling joint after joint. His house was warm and comfortable and he had pay TV. I remember walking inside from the backyard to catch the tail end of an episode of *Ren & Stimpy* and laughing so hard I thought my heart would stop. I remember how much fun I had scoffing pizza and listening to Pink Floyd's *Dark Side of the Moon* on Ben's dad's huge stereo speakers, letting the twin channels blow my tiny mind. That you could have fun smoking pot was a revelation; it was a world away from the furtive paranoia of smoking cones out of Sam's bedroom window.

Catching the train home the next day, I felt dazed and hungover, but, as I sat on the platform, I could feel the loneliness that had spread over me since childhood burn off like a morning fog. My winning combination of shyness and snobbery had made me solitary, and spending the night smoking and laughing with acerbic, witty kids my own age was a turning point. They seemed ridiculously cool; they knew music and books and the phone numbers of girls I was too timid to talk to. On top of all that, they'd insisted on paying me for the weed, and as I jumped on the train I was clutching a blushing-red $20 note.

Word got around, and classmates started calling me up to ask for weed. At first I would trade it for booze. I had made a friend, Dave, the son of a hard-drinking supermarket manager, who would exchange vodka or whisky from his parents' liquor cabinet for buds that I nicked from Mum and handed over to him raw, covered in lint from the pockets of my tracksuit.

Then I started to get hit up for grams by older kids at school, then by people outside of school, then by the wider neighbourhood. One magical day, Lilly, my eternal unrequited love, called me and asked me to meet her by the swings with a gram, which was as close to romance as I'd ever come. I was happy to oblige as I didn't think selling a little pot was a big deal.

It's easy to follow my logic. I'd grown up surrounded by those who'd smoked pot, which is illegal, and they all seemed like good people. Ergo, the laws that say you can't smoke pot don't make sense. And if those laws are bullshit, what other laws are bullshit? So I didn't have any kind of moral objection to helping people to score weed while I made a buck off it. If anything pedalling my pushbike out to meet some paranoid stranger in a bong-stinking bungalow made me feel grown-up and sophisticated. It seemed to me that what I was doing was a far less serious enterprise than my new clients thought. My new role as purveyor of illegal drugs seemed as innocuous a chore to me as picking up a paper round.

At first I stole a little at a time from my parents' stash, then, after Ardian got busted doing the same thing and was grounded, I started buying in bulk from a local dealer.

Marco had introduced me to Jimmy the Builder, an affable Turkish carpenter who made ends meet by wholesaling drugs. He was kindly and brash and never discreet, cruising around the suburbs in a specially imported Lexus while wearing work-dirty overalls. The police knew what he was up to but could never manage to catch him in the act. Every couple of days he would get pulled over by an unmarked car and would wait patiently while the cops ran their gloved fingers over his upholstery. He carried his stash, a bulging plastic bag of pills and dope, down the front of his jocks. One time a cop pointed at his groin and asked him to explain the bulge.

'Hey,' he grinned at her, grabbing at it, 'I'm Turkish!'

Jimmy would meet me out the back of the 7-Eleven, drive me

around the block in his Lexus and then sell me an ounce of weed for $300. I'd take that home and divide it into grams by sight, like a pizza maker measuring dough, so that I had twenty-eight little even buds, all in a row. I'd then wrap these up in foil and hide them in my bedroom. It took me about a fortnight to clear an ounce bag, selling each gram for $25. That made me $700, or a clear profit of $400, or 133 per cent of my initial investment. I'd never really had spending money before, and it was odd to have so much of it all of a sudden. I would count it out on my bed and look at the squirrelly pile of loose notes in wonder.

The cash didn't come easily, though. I got out of school at 3.10 p.m., went home to eat and change, and then I would be on the road, pumping the pedals on my BMX from four until late at night, making deliveries. I always made sure that I met clients at their places. Deals on the street made me nervous and when I had the chance to see how someone lived, it was easier to judge what kind of person they were: whether a client was just socially awkward or if they were visually measuring me as a fit for the chains in their dungeon.

There were very few bad scenes, all things considered. There was one time when a local gangster and semi-professional boxer thought I had ratted him out to the cops and took me for a ride in his car with a bunch of heavies. Another time, during one of those droughts when there was hardly any product to be found on the street, I followed a dodgy contact to Camberwell, into a room full of Cambodian smack dealers with sharpened machetes who stared me down and muttered in Khmer. I bought my bag of weed and did my best to smile as broadly as possible while still looking small and inoffensive, with lots of pleases and thank-yous, like a tourist trying to order coffee in Paris.

I started to move more and more weed. At first I took orders on the house phone. As I began to get calls from strangers in the middle of the night asking for product, I worried that my folks would find out what I was up to, so I bought myself a little Nokia prepaid mobile.

It's a cosmopolitan industry, really. People buy drugs for all kinds of reasons: for recreation, out of habit, as self-medication for trauma or mental illness. Loneliness was the kicker for a lot of my clients. There were the very ill, the very awkward, young divorcees and the like, who took drugs to forget their loneliness. Some bought them just for the human contact. Those housebound with a disability or agoraphobia, or who were alone in a new city, might call a dealer over, like a pizza boy, just to have a visitor for a while.

I understood this motivation; I appreciated the contact too. Often I would stay late, chatting with clients, sharing bowls of weed or packets of Twisties. The client–dealer relationship is confidential by nature and the minute I sat down many of my clients would unleash long stream-of-consciousness confessions, telling me their secrets and fears and jealousies, heart-rending, scandalous gossip about people I would never meet. It happened more often than you'd expect, apropos of nothing, this intense, one-sided intimacy. Maybe because I'd be meeting someone with the explicit purpose of trading contraband, I passed a certain threshold of privacy that encouraged people to load me up with baggage before sending me out the door: well-hidden hatred for their mum, frustrations with their partner. Perhaps mine was just a familiar but peripheral face obliged to sit through a half-hour of polite chatter, like a hairdresser's.

They told me about their sex lives, their problems at work, if they were contemplating divorce or violence or suicide. I got the feeling that in most cases I was far enough removed from their real lives that they could confide things to me they wouldn't tell anyone else. One client, the floor manager of a call centre, had dumped his girlfriend years ago but couldn't get over her.

'I know I shouldn't have done it, man,' he told me, of the time he got drunk and rode his motorbike to her place to confront her new boyfriend. 'I suppose he's a nice guy. I can see it from his point of view. If I was still with her and some ex turned up drunk in the middle of the night, I'd be upset. So I left. But as I was leaving I saw her favourite G-string lying in the middle of the hallway. When we were together, I used to get mad at her for leaving her shit everywhere but when I saw that G-string, I just got sad. Like, he's in there now, you know? And I got on my motorbike and I was going across the West Gate Bridge, and I stopped, and thought, *What if I just jumped?*'

He looked up at me for a reaction, his eyes as wide and guileless as a teddy bear's. It was a moment, the *cri de coeur* of a very unhappy man. I was fourteen, and also stupendously high, so not the best confidant.

'Oh,' I said, not entirely convincingly. 'Don't kill yourself. But if you do, can I have your bike? I mean, you aren't going to need it.'

One day he stopped calling me, which means he worked it out, one way or the other.

Running drugs got me out of the house, away from my books and my morose records. Going to party after party to make deliveries forced me to come out of my shell, and, oddly, encouraged me to smoke less weed. I started to consider myself a professional and so restricted my own smoking to when I was hanging out with friends. I wanted to stay on the ball in case things went badly.

Towards the end of the year, just as the seemingly endless Melbourne winter was starting to break, I went to a party with some older kids, where Jules and Marco knew some musicians. We were standing against a wall, flowering, sipping beers. An older girl I recognised from school came up – tall and thin with the lank, matted post–Rage Against the Machine dreadlocks that girls wore back then. She was wearing a too-tight bra that showed through a threadbare band T-shirt. I stared at her breasts, then, when she caught me, at the ground, stricken.

'I know youse,' she said. 'You guys are musos!'

Jules nodded, and Marco smiled and bantered, dropping jokes and names with easy, bleary-eyed charm while I stood by, taking notes.

'I like you guys. You guys are cool.' She smiled, and then pointed at me.

'What about you?' she asked. 'Are you cool? You're just kind of standing there.'

I wet my lips and let out a little squeak. Jules stepped in.

'This is Liam. Do you know Liam? He's a dealer.'

She turned over this information with the easy professionalism of a dad flipping a sausage on a barbecue. 'Cool.'

I liked the sound of that, especially coming from a pretty girl who'd never have noticed me otherwise. 'Yes,' I told her, 'I'm a dealer. Would you like my number?'

6

There was a double standard in play when it came to drug dealers in our house. Mum and Dad had no problem with my smoking weed, provided I did my chores, and would share spliffs with us older children on special occasions, but they were sniffy about the act of selling pot.

Actually, they were surprisingly uncool about it all when they found out I'd been selling weed. They liked smoking pot, yes, and mushrooms got a pass, but they were stridently anti-drugs otherwise, except for acid, of course, but only on holidays. I can distinctly recall a family holiday to Sydney, when Dad had booked us a hotel in Kings

Cross and was outraged to find it full of junkies once we'd arrived. They were particularly disappointed, then, one school night when I was in Year 9 when a junkie knocked on the door, looking for me.

The family was sitting around the lounge room, watching a documentary on fractal art. We were, like the brownies we'd been eating all afternoon, deliciously toasted. Hamish, who at age ten was too young for hash cake, was playing with Lego on the carpet. One of Ardian's friends had just harvested a summer crop and supplied us with a bag of weed leaf, which we'd spent the afternoon baking.

When a crop is harvested, the buds, sticky with THC-rich resin, are stored and sold, but the remaining garbage bags full of leaf, comparatively low in psychoactives, are either given away or sold for next to nothing, as with bones at a butcher's. There is very little THC in the leaf of the plant, but it can be teased out through slow cooking in margarine. It's a very thrifty way to use weed. The memory of the Potato Famine runs in our veins and if we were given a bag of terrible weed leaf then, by God, we were going to get high with it.

Hash brownies have a way of sneaking up on you. You don't realise how strong they are until it's too late. You'll munch a couple and then an hour later, thinking they haven't worked, you'll be halfway through a third when you'll start to feel a mellow lull creep up your bones, and you'll just have time to think, *Oh no!*, when suddenly you'll be able to see through time. We were sitting around, waiting for the brownies to kick in, fidgeting throughout *Neighbours*. Towards the end of *The Simpsons*, my mum started kneading her eye sockets with her knuckles and announced, 'Oh, wow. I never realised my eyeballs were so *round*. Do you think that's why they call them eye*balls*? Hey, Liam, feel my eyes.' We were ready for the movie.

Ardian had sourced a documentary from someone at uni that showed how scientists were using computer modelling to produce visual representations of chaos mathematics, interspersed with spinning CGI images of fractal equations being calculated. The film showed the psychedelic fields of numbers, plotted in colour, as weird, organic shapes flowering ever outwards, recurring again and again, before the ubiquitous shape of the Buddha would appear. All the while, a soothing voice-over explained how maths, art, science and the natural world were one and the universe was infinitely recursive and magical. For a couple of gentrifying hippies and their kids, this was a pretty big day.

Afterwards, we sat in stoned appreciation of the beauty of the world, the intrinsic interconnectivity of all matter, energy and consciousness, eating packet after packet of Tim Tams. Together we wandered through the house, giggling and bumping into tables as we spotted the fractal art that played out everywhere around us. Ardian ambled over to the hall near the front door, where one of Mum's artworks was hanging. 'Look here!' he said, in his thoughtful, gentle way. 'They're all through this picture.' We crammed into the hallway to admire the loops and swirls of Mum's artwork, which we now realised had been obviously governed by some divine higher universal truth, when the doorbell rang.

We all jumped and looked at each other, unsure of what to do. None of us was fond of police and a knock at the door this late at night was never good news. Eventually Dad opened the door. A stranger was on the doorstep, medium height, mid twenties. 'Hi!' he said to Dad. 'Can I buy some weed off you?'

Dad was quiet for a beat, and then answered slowly, with exaggerated confusion. 'What?'

'Weed.'

'I don't know what you're talking about,' said Dad unconvincingly.

'Weed,' the stranger said, then again, louder, slower and with more careful diction, like an American in an airport. 'Grams. I want to buy some pot off you.'

'I'm afraid I can't help you,' my dad said, before starting to close the door. My heart started to slide back down my throat, when an idea struck the stranger. 'Oh, I'm sorry. I must have the wrong place. Are you Liam? I wanted to buy some weed off Liam.'

Dad stopped closing the door and turned to look at me. There was a long, excruciating silence as the stranger walked inside, pushing past Dad to shake my hand.

'You must be Liam! Hope you don't mind. Your mobile was off so I thought I'd just knock on the door. Can I buy a quarter?'

'I can't help you,' I choked out.

He looked confused. 'But everyone said you could.'

'They were wrong.' I took the stranger by the arm and walked him to the door. 'I don't sell weed. I'm very sorry.' I started to close the door and gave him just enough time to yell out, 'What about pills?'

I turned back around. Mum and Dad were angry. Ardian was grinning mirthfully. I was in trouble.

There was some yelling, then some pleading, and then finally my parents sat me down for a talk. Mum spoke while Dad furiously rolled and then smoked a joint, too angry to talk, and I tried to reason my way out of this mess.

'We don't want our child to be a drug dealer,' said Mum.

'Some of your best friends are drug dealers.'

'Those aren't our friends. Those are our drug dealers.'

'They're friendly.'

'But they aren't *friends*,' she sighed, and paused, thinking for a moment. 'They are dealers − people who spend their whole lives around drugs − but they aren't necessarily people we want to know. You'll find that as you get older, if you keep taking drugs, people are going to turn their backs on you. They'll want less and less to do with drugs, and less and less to do with you. We want more for you than to be a drug dealer.'

'I'm not a drug dealer,' I said. 'I'm in high school. I just happen to deal drugs.'

Ardian stepped forward. 'It's not like you're a great student. You don't bring home the grades, and you're not really making a lot of cash from this, so you may as well give it up and do some fucking homework.'

He was only half right. I was a terrible student: precocious but also smart-arsed and lazy. I was, however, making a fortune, at least compared to my classmates. I tried to explain this to my family, starting with words before fetching a paper and pen to supply a diagram of the logistics.

I'd stepped up my operation after the first few months, when my business had expanded to the point where I couldn't handle it on my own any more. I took my ounce bags of weed and divided them into quarters to sell on to other dealers who I'd subcontracted. I would give the bags to a roster of neighbourhood burnouts who would then on-sell the product and pay me the wholesale price. It cut down on travel time and reduced my risk by some margin.

It also plumped up my little ego. I'd found that people gave me respect, or what looked very much like respect, for having the chutzpah to flout the law, and that in turn gave me the confidence to step up my game. I handed out bags of dope along with platitudes about life on the street that I'd learned from Wu-Tang records, and bristled with pride when my underlings nodded and scurried off to do my bidding.

I didn't keep weed in the house and only had it in my possession for a few hours at a time. Anything I had to hold on to for more than a day or two was stashed at a friend's place, for which I paid him a retainer. On the rare occasion I got into trouble, I had people who would sort it out for a small amount of money or else they took payment in trade.

Some of my team offered to pay me in kind: pills, bags of speed, bushels of raw tobacco they'd scored from the Philip Morris factory. While I would occasionally pass these goodies on to friends who'd asked for them specifically, they held no interest for me. I partly assumed I would learn to enjoy them once I was a little older and my tastes had matured, as with asparagus, but for now I felt too young.

I knew my parents would disapprove, and I very much wanted to make them proud of me, so I ran them through my operation. While I was showing them how much I could make in a week with just a few deals, Dad came to see things from my point of view. He was a crusading moralist at times, but a miser first and foremost. Our salad days had given him a religious appreciation for the value of a dollar, and he was magnificently thrifty. I was with him in 1992 when he lost a $50 note he'd saved to have a pair of shoes mended and, even now, whenever he glazes over with a look of Proustian sorrow, I know he's thinking about that fifty bucks.

Throughout my youth, Dad's one concession to drifting into the middle class was a keenness for the stock market. He loved the Dow Jones as only a fading liberal can, and he was good at using it to spin nothing into money. When Telstra was floated in 1997 he bought me a couple of hundred bucks' of stock and spelt out the mechanics of the market to me the way another dad might have taught his son to shave or fish or fight. Dad was a bohemian – he dressed in rags, drove a battered old Toyota Camry and only really bought books and records – but that didn't mean he didn't appreciate money. He wasn't happy that I was pushing drugs, but he admired the economics of the cottage-industry mafia I was at the helm of.

He sat down and ran through the sums with me, carefully double-checking the profit margins.

'When you buy in this amount, how much does an ounce cost you?' he asked. I named a figure.

He smiled. 'And what would it cost me?'

So I started selling weed to my parents. It worked out okay. Turns out they didn't mind that I was selling drugs as long as it looked as though I was doing my homework, I kept the gear away from the house, and I gave them easy access to cheap, good-quality weed. There's nothing worse than coming home from a hard day at work and having to meet some pissant dealer in a freezing park when all you want to do is get dinner on the table and settle in on the couch for the evening.

Keeping it in the family had its perks for me too. For one thing, they knew how to speak in code over the phone. As a rule of thumb, you want to keep any phone discussions of illegal activities vague and nebulous, or at least substitute terms such as 'drug' and 'deal' with code words. It's especially helpful if it all ends up in court. Although, in later years, criminal lawyer friends of mine would laugh themselves silly at transcripts of incongruous, hack-ish codes, such as the guy who would call his dealer late on a Saturday to order 'twenty-eight dresses'. Some clients got the hang of it fairly quickly, but I was amazed at how many people were unable to grasp the simplest code. To a client who was after ecstasy, for example, I might have said, 'Just tell me you want to borrow a CD. I'll know what you mean.' Then they would call me a few days later with, 'Hey, Liam! It's me! You know! I bought those CDs from you the other day. Anyway, I'm going to a rave this weekend and I need some CDs. Only I need a lot, so could I get maybe a ten-pack of CDs? And those last CDs were kind of speedy so could you throw in another half a CD? And also do you know where I could find a gram of coke?', by which time I'd hung up in exasperation, and the police were speeding around to my house with a battering ram.

Mum at least knew how to talk in gangster slang. Anyone who's spent a couple of decades getting high picks up the trick of talking casually about contraband. If Mum wanted to buy a bag, she would call and ask, 'Hey, Liam, have you seen my umbrella?'

To which I would reply, 'The big one?'

'No, the little one. The one your father uses at the weekend.' And I would bring home a quarter bag of grass. See how easy that is?

So helping Mum and Dad to score was ideal, as far as I could see, although it made negotiating pocket money awkward. I thought I should get more as I was dealing to them at cost price, but they didn't see it that way. In the end, I took it as an overhead. I had plenty of pocket money anyway.

Selling drugs wasn't all smiles and sunshine. Because I spent most of my time brokering deals, I never did my homework. My grades crashed and my teachers quickly went from viewing me as a bright but indolent kid to a no-good shitkicker. Not that this changed how they acted towards me: the majority of the teachers was pretty jaded and treated every kid as a no-good shitkicker. Occasionally I'd get a young, idealistic English teacher who would get excited by an essay I wrote, before realising they didn't have a *Dead Poets Society* situation on their hands and going back to having the life bled out of them and writing poetry on trams. Every maths teacher hated me right off the bat, but I didn't mind; I had the small-business owner's disdain for any maths I couldn't do on a mobile-phone calculator.

My grades only bothered me at report-card time, when my folks would get furious beyond all proportion. I never understood why: they'd raised me to be anti-establishment and, besides, I didn't really have any ambitions that required good grades.

My only real goal in high school was to get next to Lilly. My crush on her had only worsened as we inched towards the later years of high school, and while we had become friends we wanted different things from the friendship. She wanted someone with whom to drink goon and talk about putting a curse on the popular girls. I wanted her to marry me and move somewhere in the Byron shire where we could raise sheep and a couple of dozen apple-cheeked children. That was the long play but I figured I would start with some earnest kissing and finger-banging.

For her part, she let me down gently, indicating that while she would probably never feel the same way, she was happy to be my friend and to help me consume the buckets of drugs I kept under the bed, against the express wishes of my parents. My personal stash was in a battered, combination-lock briefcase, away from prying eyes and from the sticky fingers of my little brother, who was starting to appreciate the virtue of free money on demand.

In a misguided effort to impress Lilly, I'd also softened my stance on party drugs. Most lunchtimes she and I would head from school to my house, where we would eat a sandwich, drink a litre or two of cask wine, and then take a little something, usually half a pill each of ecstasy, to prop us up in that afternoon's classes.

I understood that Lilly wasn't interested in me romantically, but I was sure that if I could just kiss her the once it would change her mind. I reasoned that the best way to make that happen was to give her enough ecstasy that she'd fall in love with me by default. Everyone knows there's nothing sexier than adolescent boys sweating and grinding their jaws while they spout gibberish. It never did work out, no matter how high we got. During our lunch hours together, I'd act steamily towards her – not like a Latin romantic, more like a dumpling. I was clammy and pale, a thin white skin covering meat of dubious provenance. I learned that filling someone to the gills with ecstasy might mean they will hold hands with you, but it won't make them fall in love.

The only real outcome was that my teachers started to notice that I often came to class drunk and high. I thought I was being surreptitious, gurning and frothing at the mouth throughout remedial maths, but no one was fooled. Ms R, young and passionate about her job, asked me to stay after class one afternoon. In a low, concerned voice she questioned how much pot I was smoking.

'Oh, none!' I told her truthfully, my eyes as wide as saucers. 'None at all!' And I twitched out of the classroom as though I'd pulled off some magnificent heist.

The twice-yearly parent–teacher interviews were the only other times my parents got on my case about studying, and it was only so they could get off school grounds quickly. They hated parent–teacher night with a passion and got ready for it the same way my friends prepared to go home to their parents when they were stoned: a cup of strong coffee to sober up, Visine Clear for blood-shot eyes, a healthy spray of deodorant to cloak the smoke. Then we would drive towards the school's halogen-lit gym, in which the three of us would shuffle around, waiting to be told off by teachers. In Year 10 my geography teacher, Mr D, took my parents aside to have a frank talk.

'I'm concerned about Liam's attitude,' he said.

'We're also concerned about Liam's attitude,' said Dad. Mum nodded.

I glared at Dad. *Traitor!* I thought. *Fucking turncoat!*

Mr D went on: 'Liam doesn't seem to have the necessary curiosity about how the world works to become a decent student.'

'He has never been a curious boy,' Dad agreed wistfully.

I was livid. 'What am I supposed to be curious about?' I snapped. 'It's geography! Maps! What's to know? It's not going to change on my watch.'

Mr D swivelled to look at me with the slow, dumb malevolence of a sideshow clown head. He fixed his gaze on me. 'My primary concern is Liam's obvious disrespect for authority.'

'We've tried to teach Liam to respect authority but he's at an age when it's very hard,' said Dad. Mum was nodding so hard I was worried her head would bisect and tumble off like in a Monty Python animation.

Mr D sighed. 'That may be, but Liam is not that young any more. We're heading into VCE, and I think it may be too late for him.'

Dad turned to look at me, his eyes full of sorrow. 'I have to agree. You've left your run a bit late, Liam.'

Mum said, 'Yep.' I sat there, cowed.

Back in the car, Mum and Dad burst out laughing.

'Mr D!' crowed Dad. 'What a wanker!'

I sat in the back fuming. *I'll show them,* I thought, and upped my price on the ounce.

7

Looking back, maybe selling the occasional bag to my folks wasn't in the best interests of the family. They didn't think it was fair of me to charge them the full rate while I was living under their roof, and I didn't think it was fair that they expected discounts when the convenience of having a dealer downstairs was an unmatchable perk. It must have made raising me a fucking nightmare. It's hard to get your kid to eat their veggies when you've fallen behind on your drug debt to them.

My business also made me at least partially to blame for Hamish getting into pot. Your classic spoiled youngest child, he not only had the best toys and video games, he also never had to risk his allowance by sneaking Mum's dope or pulling the elaborate heist that required. Instead he could just pop into my room while I was out and nick as much pot and pocket money as he wanted. I had no idea, mind you. I only twigged that he even knew what weed was after the school busted him.

Hamish had only just started high school, his hand-me-down uniform still baggy on him, when he was caught selling joints on the back oval by a teacher. They called the cops, who marched him through the school, searched his locker, found his pot and arrested him in front of the milling crowd before taking him down to the station. I was struggling through a biology test when a teacher's aide stuck her head around the door to tell me they were taking Hamish to the cop shop, and could I meet him there.

He got off with a warning, but he was miffed about all the pageantry. 'They didn't have to arrest me in front of everybody. I guess they were trying to humiliate me,' he said, sighing. 'Idiots.'

If the big show of arresting him in front of his peers was meant to deter Hamish, it didn't work. Rather, the whole junior school now knew who to go to when they wanted to score weed.

While it was surprising to have to head down to the police station to sign him out, the incident seemed natural, part of life's progression, like *I think I need to start shaving*, or *I reckon the old lemon tree is on its last legs*, or *Oh, Hamish gets high now*.

Ardian was interested in my goods as well, complicating the already strained fraternal relationship, with one brother entering adolescence, one leaving it. Ardian had moved out of home and gone to university, where he was trying to cut back on weed, an almost impossible task when living in a share house with one or more arts students in it. I wasn't helping: I was a soft touch and always gave him pot when he asked. He was my brother, after all, and at any point he could have Chinese-burned me into submission.

He used to come around at weekends, loudly swear off weed and criticise me for selling drugs, which he saw as making money from other people's misery. 'You're an amoral little shit,' he would tell me. 'And karma is going to come back and bite you on the arse.' A few hours later, he would call to ask me if he could grab a gram.

'You told me not to sell you any more weed,' I'd complain. 'You were quite certain about it. You called me amoral.'

'I asked you not to sell *me* any more weed,' he'd counter, and then continue in a conspiratorial whisper. 'There's a beautiful girl here who wants to get high and spend the night with me. I want you to sell *her* a gram.' Every fiend ran that line, or something like it. There was always some extenuating circumstance that required another gram, another quarter, another time.

All my clients, sooner or later, would want drugs 'on tick', which meant 'on loan', which, between my memory not being great and my being too craven to demand payment, usually meant 'for free'. In the

end, I refused all tick out of principle. I used to envy the street push-
ers on TV who didn't have to be friends with their clients, who didn't
feel guilty about refusing somebody tick.

I lost friends over it. Or rather, not friends but people I was
friendly with; I couldn't always tell the difference. One night I was
walking back from a bad meeting with a client I'd scored for. He
was a regular, a slightly older guy who liked to take pills and stay up
playing computer games. I'd handed over the pills without thinking,
and he'd popped them there and then. Once they were safely in his
tummy, he'd told me he had no cash and that he'd pay me back the
next week. I'd argued with him some but there wasn't much I could
do, short of beating him up and taking his wallet. I'd never hit anyone
before and I wasn't about to start now. He was a nice kid but socially
awkward, the kind who lives somewhere on the autism spectrum and
at every party ends up in the kitchen, talking to the dog.

I walked home seething with rage, kicking myself for not being
more assertive. One of my drug suppliers, an experienced, well-built
guy, had given me some advice on the practice of ticking drugs. He'd
give any customer the benefit of the doubt once but the second time
they didn't pay, he would fuck them up, leave some visible bruises.
He assured me that you don't have to do it often before people get
the message. I couldn't see that working for me. I still slept with the
lights on, because of ghosts, and kept a copy of *The Hobbit* on my
bedside table. Fucking people up wasn't in my wheelhouse.

I was mulling over his words when my old buddy Sam called, asking
for tick. We'd been drifting apart for years, as I spent all my time flitting

about the suburbs and he hung out in his room, smoking cones and listening to trance. He told me that he had an exam that he was stressed out about, and he didn't have any money but just wanted enough weed to calm him down enough so he could study. It was a version of an excuse I'd heard from my brother and my parents. I lost my temper and yelled at him: he should take some responsibility for himself, not get himself into the position where he couldn't afford something he needed. He started yelling back, then crying. I laughed at Sam, telling him to call me the next day once he had got his shit together and found some money. Then I hung up. That was the last time I ever spoke to him.

That night, around 11 p.m., the client from earlier knocked on my door. His pills had worn off and he wanted some weed to come down – again, on tick. I was furious. I made it quite clear to my clients never to come near the house, but they didn't listen. I was angry but instead of the bitter, guilty anger I'd been stewing in all night, this was good, clean fury.

'Sure,' I said. 'Let's take a walk.'

We strolled together to the park, on some pretext. Halfway into the darkness, he asked where we were going.

'To have a chat.'

The penny dropped. I could see the realisation on his face, then the fear that flashed across it a second later.

'I'm not going any further,' he said. 'I'm not going anywhere if you're just going to hit me. You don't have to hit me.'

But I did. And it turned out he had the money after all.

I came to convince myself I was a gangster. I learned that nine times out of ten a fight is over once one side throws a punch. That remaining 10 per cent, though, the ones where people fight back, still had me worried. To offset the probability of having to fight, I went around telling anyone who would listen how dangerous I was. I imagined that people were looking at me with a new kind of respect, one born of fear. My walk changed from the furtive, crouched scurry of a chubby teenager trying to hide his breasts to a gangster's strut – chest puffed out, shoulders rolling from side to side with each stride, like my bulging muscles were throwing me off balance. People glanced at me, then quickly looked away. At the time I thought they were just being street smart, but the response was probably closer to confusion and pity at the chubby, ponytailed androgyne twitching down the street like a traumatised chimp who'd escaped from a Krispy Kreme research facility. But I believed I looked dangerous and that's what mattered.

Getting into an actual fight with some clients who whipped my arse and took my money in the alley behind a 7-Eleven should have been an early sign that I wasn't supposed to be a criminal. But I was stubborn, and Darwin wasn't the boss of me, and I was determined to keep plying my trade. It's not easy to think about stopping selling drugs; it can be harder than giving up using. You get used to the easy money, the endless, stress-free drug supply and the adulation of addicts, who greet you when you walk in the door with the crafty but brainless enthusiasm of a beagle.

After my first beat-down, I looked at my situation logically, dabbing antiseptic onto my cuts. I wasn't planning on going straight any time soon but I had what marketing types call a 'crisis of publicity'. Word was spreading around the neighbourhood that I was soft. If I kept going, I could expect to be ripped off and robbed time and again. The only other option, as I saw it, was to learn to fight.

I found a martial arts school in a tiny studio above a bar. I was so painfully nervous that I walked around the block three times before I stepped through the doorway of the dojo to ask about joining the club. As I climbed up the narrow stairwell the concrete echoed with a staccato crack accompanied by an angry bellow. At the top of the stairs I saw a wiry man in his sleeveless black uniform laying into a heavy punching bag with rhythmic, lightning-fast roundhouse kicks, each of which bent the bag in two. It was awesome. As I stepped across the threshold he spoke, without taking his eyes off the bag or breaking his tempo: 'You bow when you enter the dojo or I'll rip your fucking face off.' That was how I met Sensei.

The sign out the front advertised 'Mixed Martial Arts' but Sensei taught a brutal mix of street fighting, kickboxing and jujitsu. 'Most fights will end up on the ground,' he announced from the front of the class as we stood at attention in ready-stance, knees bent and fists cocked loosely at the waist. 'So when you're there just break an elbow and the fight is yours.' Sensei had honed his pragmatic fighting style over a couple of decades of petty crime, during which he alternated spells in prison with brief periods when he laundered money and taught martial arts to teenagers. He was the coolest motherfucker I'd ever met.

I hung on his every word, carefully copying his movements as he demonstrated kicking techniques, and aping the way he hissed when he kicked the heavy bag. He spoke to the part of me that left each Spiderman film pretending I could shoot webs from my fingers when nobody was watching. In a way that must have been obvious to everybody in the room but me, I started to model my behaviour on Sensei's.

He was a little more than 6 foot but seemed taller: lean and long like he'd been threaded together out of high-tension rope. He was pushing forty but had the angry energy of a much younger man. Whenever he was forced to sit still he would seethe and bob, jiggling a knee against the floor, rolling his shoulders or bunching up a fist to crack his knuckles against his temple. Only his receding hairline gave away his age, that and a few lines around his temples, framing the same watchful, baleful eyes I'd seen belonging to a caged cockatoo.

None of that bothered me. The fact that he could kick through a brick wall was all I needed to know about him. I was a teenager and casting about for a more accessible authority figure than those already around. I didn't feel comfortable going to my own dad with problems about girls, schoolwork or troublesome clients; when he was feeling frivolous he liked to make jokes about Camus. Sensei gave me a more relatable role model.

Three times a week Sensei taught me the ins and outs of real-life combat situations, which I took in as catechism. 'I'll show you how to kill a man with one punch. Grab me here,' I urged my friends. 'No, no. *Here.*' After a few weeks of classes, one of the better students approached me as we stretched down. 'Oi,' he said by way of introduction, 'do you choof?' That was how I met the Ryans.

The Ryans were a group of siblings who all trained at the club, all lived together in a house around the block and all smashed cones after class with the grim determination normally seen in athletes. They had names like Arlen and Molloy, and shared the same broadly Irish features and dirty-blond Kurt Cobain hairdo. I was never sure who were actual Ryans and who had just moved into the share house and become Ryans by osmosis. There was only one female, Di, a sandy-haired, tough-talking teenager who could hold her own with the rest of the boys as they smoked themselves into stupors and told filthy, violent stories. I quickly became hopelessly infatuated with her.

Happy months passed in which I spent almost no time at home. My parents seemed pleased that I'd taken an interest in sport and encouraged me to take Hamish along to the club, an idea that I bucked against. I didn't want him tagging along to spoil the fun with my new friends and, besides, I didn't want him to learn how to fight as well as me. I was proud of my developing muscles and high kicks and the fact that for the first time I could, if I so chose, whoop my big brother's arse. I wasn't about to let an upper hand like that go.

I would fidget my way through school, leap around the gym doing fly kicks and grapples after hours, and then go home with the Ryans to have competitive bong races and eat microwave schnitzels. Between the martial arts training and the Ryans' companionship, I changed. I got leaner, stronger and faster, and I started to flirt, in my own awkward way, with Di. When the Ryans got hyped up on cones lightly sprinkled with meth and started practising knife fighting, I would steal off to Di's room. There we'd share bourbon and Coke from a can and I'd listen to her dissect Slim Shady lyrics in rambling, profound exegeses.

We became close, quickly. When business called she would keep a lookout while I did deals in the alleyway. It was all very nice. It was the first time I had ever really felt comfortable around a girl. In my eyes, any kind of romance was off the table, in large part due to the half-dozen siblings in the next room who were all trained to kill. That lack of sexual tension let me relax and become something other than the skittish, uneasy weirdo I normally was around the opposite sex.

One night when we were drunk, she walked me to the door, leaned over and kissed me lightly on the lips. I was stunned, moving and thinking slowly, as she leaned back and smiled at me, suddenly shy herself. Her hair fell over her face as she looked across and said goodnight. The door closed. As the lock snicked gently into place I woke up. I raised a hand to knock, then put it down again. As I walked home and all through the next day I could feel her lips against mine, like the afterimages a candle burns at the backs of your eyes.

Di invited me to a party at the Ryan Palace one weekend. It was a big deal to me: the parties at the Ryans' were infamous. People got into fights at those parties. People got stabbed. People got laid. So I made an effort. I usually wore my hair long and ragged but that night I brushed it and tied it back in a ponytail, and I washed my best hoodie. I was jittery with nerves when I walked in, all the more so when I found Sensei sitting at the kitchen table.

'These cunts tell me you're a fucking dealer!' he yelled, pointing a finger at me. I was mortified. He bounced over, took my arm and hustled me outside, where it was quiet.

'Word is you're a bit of a hardcore,' Sensei said, punching me affectionately on the shoulder. 'Stick with me, kid. I'll make you rich. Whatever you want. Weed? I got weed. Pills? I can get 'em for you, three bucks a pop. No problem. I'll look after you, kid. Whatever you need.'

My little heart swelled.

'Seriously, kid. You ever need anything. You need somebody's head kicked in? You only need to ask. You're a mate. I look after my mates.'

After that I hung out with Sensei a fair bit. There was an unspoken demarcation between Sensei the teacher, Monday to Friday, stern and upstanding, and Sensei the mate, who I'd see on weekends at the Ryans'. One weekend he saw me glance longingly at Di from across the room.

'You like her, don't ya?'

I admitted that yes, I did, but I couldn't say anything to her. She was a Ryan and I wouldn't want to damage my friendship with the family.

'You won't, guaranteed. I fucked her,' he said helpfully. 'I fucked her in the butt.'

He made a strange gesture: a loose uppercut that he terminated by opening his fist and pursing his fingers into a steeple, then splaying them out like an Italian grandma illustrating something delicious. The action perturbed me. What did he mean? Did his penis taper off and unfurl like a tulip? Did it explode outwards into a grappling hook like a cat's?

He laid a paternal hand on my shoulder. 'She's a great root. You should have a stab. She loves it. She's a massive slut, honest.'

Sensei was full of advice. He'd train me in combat, and once in a while he'd teach me a little about the world. He showed me how to cut a bag of speed with a benign agent to make the dollar stretch further. Sensei advocated glucose energy powder, which had the same weight, volume and texture as fine powdery speed. The trick was to cut it down to a 70 per cent speed–30 per cent neutral mix.

'Any more than that and people will be able to taste it when they rub it into their gums. Any more than *that* and they may as well be snorting NutraSweet.'

He taught me how to fight but, more importantly, he promised that next time I got into trouble he would drop whatever he was doing and head down to sort it out. I'd seen Sensei take a baseball bat to the arm and shrug it off like an insult before snatching the weapon from his assailant and choking him unconscious with it. It felt good to know he was on my side.

Sensei never actually intervened in any of my conflicts, but the knowledge that he could kept me out of trouble. I had the sort of swagger that only a little man with the ability to summon divine retribution can muster. I came further out of my shell; I refined my personality, turned my shyness into a sword. When I got into a confrontation with a pushy client, I would let my voice level drop to a fell whisper, lean in close and murmur threats in their ear almost tenderly. I changed myself from a bashful pusher into a psychotic dwarf who seemed likely to fly off the handle given the slightest push. Of course, I never had to. The thing about fighting is that the more you act like you can, the less you'll have to. My swagger saw me through, thank God. I was rarely called on to fight. That didn't stop me thinking that I could, though.

I carried a flick-knife in the back pocket of my jeans. When I thought the situation would be particularly dicey, I slid a trolley pole up the sleeve of my jacket. I never thought too hard about what it might be like to have to use my weapons; they were just part of my outfit. Arming myself was just something I did before I left the house, like gelling my hair.

My rounds grew too time-consuming and far-ranging for me to deliver by foot or pushbike, so I hired a driver. Sunny was in his early twenties, a waiter at the casino with a lisp and a taste for the finer things in life. I'd flip him a bag of drugs or a few bucks and he would drive me around all night while we talked crime, bumped Dr Dre through the subwoofers and stared down teenagers from the windows of his Mazda 323. In between rolling blunts with the shells of vanilla cheroots, we passed the time with him lecturing me on the correct way to listen to hip-hop.

'A crib is a house, and a shorty used to mean someone young or new to the game, but since you white people have started listening to rap it's come to mean a fine-bodied female,' he would say. 'You'll find that a lot of terms have changed since rappers started pandering to suburban America. Like the word "nigger". When nigger first started being used in rap it was a deliberate effort to reclaim the word from the oppression of white racists. I would be proud to use the word nigger. Now its use by Ja Rule and other establishment tools has diminished its impact to the point where it's a tool of oppression again. When whitey started listening to rap it stopped being the music of liberation and became a yoke for the black man again.' Sunny was Indian, incidentally.

Sunny stole one of his dad's hunting rifles, a lever-action Winchester .22, which had escaped John Howard's purge in the wake of the Port Arthur massacre and wound up in the boot of Sunny's car, wrapped in a picnic blanket. Occasionally, when I wanted to impress someone, I would walk them around to the back of Sunny's car and throw the blanket back to show the rifle, its barrel gleaming red in the brake lights. I'd grin and raise one eyebrow to convey my meaning: 'Look! It's a gun! It's for shooting!'

Between my weapons and the shadowy promise of protection from Sensei, I felt pretty good about myself. He boosted my confidence and helped me to be a better criminal, but the way he really changed my life was by getting me drugs. He got me lots of drugs, really good drugs, at really good prices. He was extremely well connected, with associates from all across Melbourne. I would meet him in the Ryans' kitchen and hand over a fat roll of money and he would return a couple of hours later with bags of product. He was like the Aldi of narcotic wholesale. On top of the huge stinking bushels of Adelaide hydro I bought from him, he lovingly catalogued the other specials he could do me: crystalline sacks of dirty brown bikie speed, delicate vials of pristine liquid LSD, festive bags of multicoloured pills.

The drugs that Sensei brought me changed my business. They were cheap and they were amazing, so much so that I stopped taking them altogether. They interfered with my training, and some part of me, the reptilian survival instinct, recognised that if I indulged in drugs this cheap and this good so young in life, I would wake up in ten years' time wearing fishnets on an LA sidewalk.

Ardian had a truism he liked to roll out whenever he had a captive audience: drugs were a window, not a door. I was starting to see it differently, though. Through Sensei I realised how lucrative the whole thing could be if I applied myself, and the first part of that meant staying away from the product. Between Sensei's leading example and my hip-hop records that exhorted me not to get high on my own supply, I stopped indulging. I didn't want to risk losing the good thing I had going. Money was more important to me than getting high, but being respected by the people I worked with was more important to me than anything.

The money was rolling in and I got cocky as I started turning over thousands of dollars a month. For a long time I'd been in the habit of smoking and drinking whatever money I made with Di and the Ryans, but as the summer approached I hoarded my cash to stock up for Christmas.

The Christmas and New Year period is the harvest season for drug dealers, as cashed-up tradies and professionals let their hair down and spend a few days getting blissfully toasted. I'd learned from the previous Christmas how quickly your stock could run out, so I'd asked Sensei to sort me out with an order large enough to see me through the summer. I met him at Castle Ryan and handed him an envelope full of ATM-fresh notes. He shoved the envelope absent-mindedly into his back pocket, winked and loped out the door on his rangy, lethal legs.

Four hours passed before I called him and got his voicemail. I tried again an hour later and found his phone switched off. Around two in the morning I went home to bed; I had school in the morning. I didn't hear back from Sensei for a week, and even then that was only because Di had given me his gym bag filled with a change of clothes and a pair of electronic scales he'd left at the Ryans'. I took that home with me and a few hours later got a text from his mobile: **YOU SNEAKY CUNT HOW DARE YOU TOUCH MY PROPERTY FUCK WITH ME AND YOULL GET THE HORNS**.

It wasn't a soothing message. I thought of the first time I'd laid eyes on Sensei, when he'd broken the heavy bag in half with his roundhouse kicks. I decided I didn't need '**THE HORNS**'. At the same time, though, I needed my product – my customers were getting restless, and I wasn't the same defenceless kid I was all those months ago. I texted back: **Hello Sensei. Where's my money?**

There was a pause of about three minutes while I sat watching the phone in my hand. I made myself breathe evenly. Then he texted me the address of an abandoned servo in the eastern suburbs, and a time.

That night I loaded the .22 and Sunny and I drove to the meet. I slipped my knife into my pants and hid my trusty trolley pole in the gap between the passenger-side seat and the handbrake. I wasn't anticipating violence but I was ready for it. As we pulled into the car park of the defunct servo, I looked for Sensei's battered Holden and saw that we were alone. He was late. I swore and rolled down the window to light a cigarette, and Sensei's face thrust through the opening.

He was very, very angry and very, very high. His jaw was grinding and his eyes were massive, empty and glazed black. His face was centimetres from mine and, with his receding hairline, big black eyes and lips pulled back in fury as he snarled abuse at me, he resembled a very fast, impossibly cross cartoon kangaroo.

'You little shit!' Specks of spit hit my face as he yelled. 'What fucking right do you have to touch my shit? Where's my bag? Step out of this car and I'll kick the fucking shit out of you!'

On the drive over, I'd carefully rehearsed how the scene was going to play out. He would threaten me, I would issue a snappy retort and be vaguely menacing in my soft-spoken way. He would apologise and give me my product, maybe even give my money back, and the world would continue turning.

Instead, I shrank and thrust his bag at him, not unlike the way you might shove a crucifix at a vampire, and squeaked, 'You disappeared! This is collateral.'

He snatched the bag from me, unzipped it and checked the contents. I pushed my luck. 'Where's my money?'

It was the wrong thing to say. 'Your money's gone!' He was screaming, his voice echoing around the empty servo. 'It was gone the second you touched my fucking stuff. You hear me? *My stuff.* You don't touch *my stuff.*' He flung the bag onto the concrete and kicked it. He stamped on it a few times for emphasis. I could hear his possessions cracking under his boots. 'You don't *touch my fucking stuff.*'

He reached in through the window to grab me by the collar and instinctively I leaned back. My hand went to the handbrake for balance and his eyes followed to where the trolley pole was resting. 'You sneaky little cunt,' he hissed, and pulled me through the window.

He banged my head once against the roof of the car and I went limp. I would have fallen had I not been held firmly around the neck by the ridge of his forearm. *It's a sleeper hold,* I thought as his hand discovered the knife in the waistband of my pants where I had tucked it. Sensei laughed as he flicked out the blade. As he pressed the point into the back of my skull I felt my bladder go. *It's a sleeper hold.* My mind fumbled for the counter grapple. I thought about the gun, lying uselessly in the boot, wrapped in a picnic blanket. Curiously, I wondered whether I'd left the milk out when I'd made tea earlier in the day. *If I left it out, it'll be spoiled in this heat,* I thought, and also, *I've wet myself.*

'You're a boy, Liam. Just a boy playing a man's game,' Sensei told me, and I realised I'd heard something similar before. It took me a minute to locate the memory. When we were children living in Oakleigh, Mum had used a big, seventies-style plastic juicer to make orange juice every morning. It was the kind where you put in whole fruit and vegetables and razor-sharp blades would tear them apart. One day, when I was around four, and thirsty for juice but not understanding how the machine worked, I stuck my hand into the juicer. Mum, who'd been in the shower, stepped out to find me screaming and holding up a mangled hand with strips of flesh hanging off it like the fronds of a jellyfish. She drove me to the hospital in her bathrobe, her hair still dripping wet, running every red light. On the way home, once I'd been stitched up and it was clear that I wasn't going to lose any fingers, she was audibly relieved but still exasperated and scared. 'You should never play with grown-up things, Liam. You're just a boy and so many adult things can hurt you.'

Sensei didn't sound exasperated or scared. He was mad, spittle foaming across my shoulders as he barked, 'Now you're going to get back in your little fucking car. And if I ever see you again I'm going to use this knife to fuck you in the arse. And if your little friend there doesn't stay in his seat until I'm gone, he gets the same. You got it?'

I nodded and winced, feeling the knife against my brainstem. 'Good,' Sensei said. A car pulled up and he climbed into it, but I didn't see him go. I was scrabbling for the Mazda's door. Once I was inside, Sunny started laughing hysterically.

'That,' said Sunny, 'was one scary nigger.'

Sunny drove me to the Ryans', where they gave me a bourbon. My hand was shaking so badly the ice in the drink sounded like a tiny wind chime. When I told the Ryans what had happened they shook their heads in collective disapproval.

'You dumb cunt,' one said. 'You shouldn't have given Sensei that much cash upfront. He's a gambling addict. It'll all be gone on the pokies by now. You won't see it again.'

I never went back to training. The thought of running into Sensei was enough to panic me. I needn't have bothered; he left the club a few weeks later. A few weeks after that, Di announced she was pregnant and that she was moving in with Sensei.

Soon I drifted away from the Ryans. I borrowed money and rebuilt my business from the ground up, selling gram bags to schoolkids. A year after my meeting with Sensei, a rumour reached me that he'd gone on a bender and disappeared, leaving Di to move back in with the Ryans, where they stayed home and smoked cones and took turns to play Tekken and rock the baby while he slept.

8

After Sensei handed my arse to me at that servo, I redoubled my efforts to make myself more threatening. I spent my days pumping iron and jogging, pushing around smaller men, who weren't easy to find, and just generally indulging in gangster fantasies. I dreaded losing out in another physical confrontation and so I adjusted my business practices to be as surly and menacing as possible. I stopped hanging out with clients and started collecting old debts. I threw caution to the wind and openly threatened recalcitrant clients over the phone. It never occurred to me that this might get me arrested.

Here's the thing about humans. If you are deluded enough, if you devote all your resources to perpetuating the ridiculous, tenuous lie that you've built your life on, you can make it work. I surrounded myself with people who would buttress the illusion that I was very dangerous indeed: sycophants and low-rent thugs who I could buy with small amounts of cash or weed. Sometimes they would ask me to join them for a puff, but I always said no. I didn't like the way it made me feel any more. The giddy euphoria I remembered from when I was a kid was gone. Instead, dark, paranoiac thoughts crashed through my brain. After a few puffs my bluster would leave me, supplanted by insecurities about how fragile my little empire was. So instead I drank spirits, and listened to west-coast hip-hop.

With the zeal that only reformed smokers have, I started to judge those who still smoked. I shook my head at my old friends who got so wasted they decided to skip parties to stay home and watch soccer on television, and sighed condescendingly when Mum finished doing yoga in front of a *Star Trek* re-run and offered me a blast of her celebratory smoke. 'No, thank you. I've quit, don't you know. Oh! You've got a hash pipe! How quaint.' I saw weed as insufferably daggy, a cantrip for the elderly and the callow.

I stopped thinking of my clients as friends, and started treating them as livestock: Jessie the unhappy punk-musician could be milked for $180 a week, James the awkward engineer for a healthy $250. This shift wasn't entirely mercenary; I just couldn't stand to be around stoned people any more. Their slow-moving lifestyles, the weekend-long video-game binges, the glacial philosophical sessions that I'd once adored pained me now. I grew short-tempered and curt with the meandering mannerisms of hippies, and, one by one, I cut off people who contradicted my reinvented Ayn Randian world view. I sealed myself in a chrysalis of hubris and self-aggrandisement, and waited for my metamorphosis into a real, grown-up criminal.

I spent less and less time at home, killing hours driving around with Sunny, building up my business again. Slowly I amassed cash, in rolls of crumpled twenties I tied up with rubber bands and hid about the house. I started to skip a lot of school, at first to make longer runs, and then, when I realised how easy it was to get away with it, just because I was lazy. None of my teachers seemed to have anything to say that I could use in life, and I didn't see how going on to university was going to help.

Ardian had got halfway through a science degree in which he'd drifted from biology to archaeology to geology, before finally dropping out to work odd jobs and concentrate on his music. He moved into a new share house a couple of suburbs over and threw his twenty-first birthday party there, where my family kicked around the backyard with his friends, tripping on acid and watching the fire-twirlers. At some point, my dad cornered Ardian to ask him when he thought he'd be going back to uni.

'I don't see the point,' Ardian said. 'There's nothing there they can teach me.' He seemed resigned to this fact, but I was excited because this gave me a precedent. It looked like Ardian was having the time of his life tooling about Melbourne, playing keys in jam bands. Sometimes my friends and I would head around to his place, where they would smoke pot and we would all listen to jazz records. The first few times I was chuffed, but, slowly, I started to make excuses not to go. In my eyes Ardian was still a perfect bohemian and a role model, but the finest of fault-lines were starting to show in my hero-worship.

The on-again off-again romance he'd enjoyed with his high-school sweetheart Callie was off again, and he was, to my dismay, sad. Most times I saw him he hit me up for weed, which I started to give him for free. I suddenly felt embarrassed that my older brother was asking for tick or a loan of $20. It jarred with my world view to think someone could be grown-up and independent and cool and still be unhappy. Sometimes I would visit and he wouldn't say anything for an hour; he'd just sink further into his big, leather armchair while Billie Holiday played on repeat. Other times he would greet me at the door, literally bouncing with excitement while he rattled on about books he had read or concerts he had seen.

He became fixated on Lupin III, a suave cat burglar from a manga series we used to watch, and started planning criminal heists of the kind he'd seen in the movies. Using a pencil and a napkin, he sketched out a plan to steal a shop display of mini-disc players by tunnelling through the wet wall of an electronics store with a rock pick left over from his geology class. Grinning maniacally, he asked me if I wanted 'in on the caper'. 'Of course!' I said, which made him enthusiastic, until his mood crashed and he became morose. 'Oh, I'm a bad person, you know? That I would steal from some businessman to make myself rich? At their expense? Don't ever be like me.'

For the first time in my life, I was beginning to think that I didn't want to grow up to be like my older brother. His moods threw me; I could never predict which Ardian I was going to get when he opened the door. And when he lapsed into one of his misty-eyed reveries about his inherent badness, I felt like laughing in his face. 'You're not bad!' I wanted to say. 'I'm the real deal. I've been in fights and I've got scars! Look at them! LOOK!'

I don't think I'd ever seen Ardian hit anyone, apart from me when we were little. He would dole out Chinese burns or Stop Hitting Yourselves, or the dreaded Typewriters, where he would pin down my shoulders with his knees and tap on my sternum with his index fingers and I would scream and plead for him to stop and he would cheerfully yell, 'I can't! We're on DEADLINE!'

I could only think of one time of late when he had lost his temper. My buddy Marco had lit a cigarette while reclining in an armchair. Ardian, who had been playing piano, wheeled around and leaped across the room. He reached under the chair and upended it, spilling Marco onto the floor. 'I said no smoking!' he roared. 'You motherfucker! NO SMOKING!' All present shrank against the walls, unsure where this fury had come from. 'GET OUT!' he screamed. 'Everyone get the fuck out!' We scuttled away, although Ardian's apoplectic rage had quickly subsided and he'd become tearful and apologetic.

'Well,' we all agreed, as we caught the train home, 'that was weird.'

Ardian had always been weird but in the best possible way. While each of us Pieper children was a little askew, he wore it the best. I remember the moment at the start of adolescence when I came to the unhappy realisation that I was an odd kid and would never be cool. When Ardian realised that about himself, rather than let it get him down, instead of sweating it, he went and started a band.

His friends, who were legion and chiefly starry-eyed young women, couldn't talk about him without using the terms 'very special' or 'life-changing'. The thing is, it remains impossible to describe him without using some kind of revolting new-age argot. As a teenager, he really did seem like an old soul, at once wise beyond his years and touchingly naive about life and its consequences.

Even as he rounded his twenties, there was something other-worldly about him, a quality reflected in the way he lived. I couldn't really imagine him ever working in an office, and neither could he. When I'd ask him what he planned to do with his life, he'd talk about starting a fully sustainable, off-the-grid commune in Tasmania.

His moods were increasingly erratic. He would have manic jags where he would leave the house in the morning and walk back in come evening, holding an aquarium full of fish and trailing a pretty girl he'd met on the train on the way from an acting audition he'd decided to attend on the spur of the moment. Then there'd be days when he didn't leave the house at all. He'd just sit in the lounge room, smoking cigarettes, inhaling nitrous oxide from a 1000-litre canister he'd scored from a dentist and watching daytime TV. Whether he was up or down, he was always getting thinner and he had dark circles where the sleep deprivation pooled under his eyes.

He'd taken a job as a night nurse at a care facility for people with severe brain injuries. He would sleep in a little room there until he was awoken by screaming, then he'd get up to change sheets soiled with drool and vomit and shit and blood, clean up the patient as best he could and try to calm them down. As the weeks went by he became more and more withdrawn, less prone to upswings, more consistently down.

One of the head nurses took a liking to him and started giving him day shifts, which meant taking the higher-functioning patients out on excursions. He was given a wheelchair-accessible vehicle and a list of approved activities, but after a couple of trips to the zoo and the Pancake Parlour, Ardian decided he could show them a better time at his place. He started bringing patients home, where they would garden or sit in the lounge room with Ardian and his house-mates, watching *Oprah* and jugging the nitrous. I visited once to find a heavy-set forty-something in pyjamas screaming in delight while Ardian popped N_2O and sang a little tune. The patient seemed to be having the time of his life, but when the care facility found out they didn't see it that way and Ardian was fired.

One afternoon I dropped in and he was sitting in the watery sun-light of his front yard, next to his motorcycle. He loved that machine, a tinny 110cc postie bike that he'd won at a government auction and fixed up to zip around town. It had maybe six moving parts but he lovingly oiled and tuned every one of them, and chromed and buffed the rest. Today the bike was totalled, scratched all up one side from an accident.

'Oh, shit, no!' I said in dismay when I saw it. 'What happened?'

Ardian slowly turned his gaze to focus on the bike, then me. He didn't say anything.

I tried again. 'So? How's work?'

'They fired me.'

'Oh . . . Well . . . No more night shifts at least, right?'

Now his eyes locked on mine. 'I don't know why they don't just kill them, Liam,' he said. 'I really don't. It would be so much kinder.' I left shortly after, spooked.

Then he disappeared. One day he just vanished from Melbourne, skipping out on his housemates, leaving his room as it was the morning he'd left the house, the rent unpaid. Nobody could tell us where he'd gone: old girlfriends hadn't seen him, and he had drifted away from many of his old friends. My parents were worried sick and made frantic phone calls to police, friends, former teachers, but nobody knew anything. Then, after a month or so had passed, we received a postcard from Byron Bay. In it, he wrote fondly about the family, saying even though he was missing us, he couldn't come home just yet because the energy of the Byron sky was just too beautiful. His sign-off was sweet if slightly defensive: 'I love you guys. It might sound like I'm tripping but I'm not tripping. I'm not.'

Ardian turned up again a few weeks after that, driving a kombi van full of Canadian hippies he'd met up north. He pulled into the driveway of his old share house unannounced to discover that his room had been given to someone else. Undeterred, he and a she-hippie he'd hooked up with on the drive down started living in the van in the driveway, until his former housemates finally had enough and asked him to find somewhere else to park his home.

Still, he came back energised from his time up north, showing off new philosophies and tricks with his firesticks. When I asked him where he'd been, he shrugged and said, 'On a caper.'

He found a new share house with a bunch of Goths and moved his possessions in: lava lamp, milk crates full of books and CDs, and a mattress covered in stains, some sinister, some jolly. The new place was the kind of hellish, cold, dark, beige-carpeted share-house purgatory that Melbourne throws up now and again, but Ardian seemed happy there. He quit smoking and started working out; when he saw us he would run to the wall, grinning like a child, to show me how many handstand push-ups he could do. I was glad he was on the up again, although I didn't understand where it was coming from all of a sudden.

I couldn't understand either how Ardian had let himself become so downhearted. He'd had the same opportunities to be happy as I had, and I was doing fine. By cleaning out my clientele and cutting away the deadwood, I'd revitalised the business and was dealing mainly with wealthy university students, who paid premium rates and on time. Plus they were fun to talk to, drove nice cars, and the girls were cute and flirtatious. I could pull off my ridiculous gangster dress-up when dealing with those cloistered private-school milklings, wreathing myself in bluster and bullshit, which is what they were looking for anyway.

Ardian called one night as I was heading out the door to visit a party full of moneyed, rebellious schoolkids. Sunny had just buzzed me to get into the car when the landline rang.

'Hey, Liam.'

''Sup?'

'What are you up to?'

'Nothing much. Just about to head out.'

'Cool . . .' He trailed off.

'How can I help, bro?' I wandered over to the mirror to check out my reflection. I looked good, but I thought I would look even fiercer if I could grow a little stubble.

'Just wanted to talk.'

'You know I don't do credit any more.'

'Nah, that's okay.'

'So what's up?'

'Just wanted to know if you wanted to hang out some time?'

'Sure. I'm busy for the next few days but I can do something this weekend.'

'That would be nice.'

'Rad. See ya then.'

'Liam . . .'

'Yeah, what's up?' I said. Sunny tooted impatiently outside.

'You've been a good brother.'

'Sure, man. Whatever. You too.'

I hung up and went out for the evening. That night at one of the parties I met a guy who asked if I could help him out some time. He was muscled and skin-headed, and I got a bad police-y vibe from him but he promised me he wasn't a cop. He had money and I was greedy for clients. I gave him my number and address and told him to pop by any time.

The next morning I was startled out of sleep by someone pounding on the door, which was just a few metres away from my bedroom. I was slightly hungover and lay swaddled in my sheets, wondering who would be around this early on a weekend. The knock came again, each purposeful thump reverberating around my room. I heard Mum walk up to the door, slide back the latch on the peephole, and then swear. She burst into my room and hissed, 'It's the cops! Hide your stash!'

It took me all of half a second to bounce across the room and grab my bag, scales and cash. I cast about frantically for a minute before deciding to shove everything down the back cushion of the sofa at the foot of my bed, and then sat down on top of it to hyperventilate. I waited, trying to calm my breathing, while I heard my mum open the front door. A muffled exchange was followed by the sound of the police moving past my door to the kitchen.

This was good. If Mum could keep them distracted long enough, I could sneak out of the house to dispose of the contraband. I was plotting the escape course in my mind, thinking of a route that would avoid the line of sight of any police cruisers parked on the street, when Mum started screaming. She screamed and screamed and screamed. It took me a moment or two to work up the bottle to enter the kitchen, where an older policeman was awkwardly hugging Mum. As it happens, they weren't there to arrest me but to break the news that Ardian was dead.

③

FANTASYLAND

9

Not long after Ardian was born, Grandma and Grandpa Pieper left the family. Grandpa had never approved of his son's bohemian lifestyle and the birth of a bastard was just too much for him. He sold the milk bar he'd run on Hawthorn Road, wrote Dad out of the will, cut his ties with Melbourne and took off with Grandma in a campervan to see Australia. The plan was to drive around the country until they found somewhere they wanted to live out their twilight years. They ended up in Kalbarri, a small town seven hours' drive from Perth, where they bought a tiny museum called Fantasyland.

I had the impression that Grandpa was never great with kids.

He strove to be your typical postwar Aussie bloke, fond of war stories, folk songs and sport. His one great ambition in life was for his two sons to become VFL footballers, and when my uncle became an artist and my dad a pot-smoking, guitar-playing poet-type, he despaired that he'd raised a pair of queers.

Grandpa had a certain world view, one that fitted nicely over the neat suburban lattice of Melbourne in the sixties. Dad, for his part, was convinced that the world had more to it than could be seen from behind the counter of the Caulfield milk bar. He found clues that there might be things more wonderful and terrible than orderly rows of lollies and canned beans, in the waves of Greek and Italian immigrants who annexed the city's corner shops, in the British and American pop that flooded the radio, in the disturbing realisation of what the numbers tattooed on the forearms of their ageing Jewish customers meant.

Dad went looking for that wider world and, as the seventies happened, he experimented with drugs, literature and music, none of which pleased his father. Grandpa was mulishly utilitarian: he went to church, for example, but only as a civic duty, eschewing the spiritualism and changing denomination – from Methodist to Baptist to Presbyterian – whenever he and Grandma moved town or decided they just didn't like the minister.

When his and Grandma's travels took them to Kalbarri, they took a tour of Fantasyland. As Grandpa wandered through the eclectic mess of exhibits, he fell in love with the place. Behind glass cases there were chunks of meteorite, a melted jug from the Hiroshima bombsite, an aviator's cap from World War One that was thought to have belonged to the Red Baron. In the backyard was a long-defused naval mine, on which some prankster had painted an atomic symbol before floating it down the river into town shortly after World War Two ended. In the basement was a simulated opal mine, a life-sized diorama of men at work digging up precious stones. The museum, a cobbled-together collection of beautiful junk, was a celebration of the Australia that Grandpa had always yearned for, blokey and whole-some but also twee and manageable. He even liked the 'Dolls of the World' exhibition, which, with its porcelain geishas and gollywogs in Fijian grass skirts, confirmed his view of the world.

After the tour, my grandparents got talking to the owner. Fantasyland was founded in 1970 by a local called Cliff Ross, who used to drum up business by feeding fish to the pelicans that gathered on the beach every morning. When tourists driving through the town would stop to check out the pelicans, Ross would delicately nudge them over the road to Fantasyland. He was very persuasive. By the end of the conversation with my grandparents, they'd agreed to use their retirement funds to buy the museum.

They stayed in Kalbarri, with Grandma running the museum while Grandpa enjoyed the retirement he'd always wanted: fish-ing, jogging and playing tennis with the local fishermen. The latter had typically made a fortune in lobsters and spent their days drink-ing homebrew and smoking weed, which they grew in secluded groves further down the coast. If my grandfather, who had decried all forms of drug abuse, understood why his new friends were so red-eyed, relaxed and easily amused by his jokes, he didn't let on. After a lifetime of wanting the Australian idyll, he'd ended up in a Tim Winton novel. He lived there very happily during his final decade. In 1990, on his doctor's orders, he'd gone to Perth to have a heart operation. Contrary to medical advice to take it easy, he drove back to Kalbarri a couple of days after going under the knife, and he was playing tennis when he had a fatal stroke.

Dad travelled across the country to bury him. I went with him, as Hamish was too young, and Ardian was too old to take time off school. We flew to Perth, then took an overnight bus to Kalbarri, where I saw Grandma for the first time since I was a toddler. She met us at the bus stop and drove us to her flat above the museum. Pelicans whirled overhead as she helped us unpack our bags.

While she and Dad handled the grown-up end of things, Grandma brought me a chocolate milk, which I sipped as I wandered through Fantasyland. Some rooms, like the small dank chamber filled entirely with those cracking porcelain dolls, filled me with a visceral dread.

Grandpa was cremated and his ashes scattered into the river that ran through town. Dad and I returned to Melbourne, and Grandma stayed on in Kalbarri for a few more years, until she was overcome with loneliness and returned to Melbourne to be near her sons. Before she left, she went down to the river to scoop up a jar of mud so that she would have some reminder of her husband.

Fifteen years later, we scattered her ashes in the ocean where she and Grandpa once loved to snorkel.

Ardian's ashes are stored in an urn at my parents' house. He was cremated the day after the funeral, and about a week after they found him where he'd overdosed on his share-house couch. Our optimism about his new leaf was misplaced, as it turned out. We didn't know that some of his friends dabbled in heroin, but, to be fair, we hadn't known about Ardian's half decade–long flirtation with it either.

He'd first tried it in high school, in a house on Centre Road where teenagers went to shoot up and listen to records, although I only found that out many years later, from those teenagers who are now grown and have children of their own. It was the nineties and that's what you did to be edgy: go to town to take in a matinee of *Eraserhead,* score a cap at the arcades on Russell Street and head home to shoot it. Since then, he'd been on and off it, using less often when things were good, more when things were bad.

Shortly before his final night, he'd bought a bunch of smack with the idea of weaning himself off it for good. He was piecing his life back together and that meant getting off the gear. He had a long-running promise to Callie, with whom he was trying to patch things up, not to touch the stuff, and he'd been clean for a month. He decided to give the last of his stash away to his housemates, who'd never tried it before. He got out his works – needle, spoon, syringe – then they chickened out and went to bed.

Ardian, who'd already had a few bourbons, sat for a little while. He called me to chat, but I was racing out the door on a job. He hung up. In the end he decided not to let the cook go begging and shot up what he had left. Waste not, want not.

This is how heroin kills you. Opiates are, among other things, respiratory inhibitors. The more opiate in your system, the shallower your breathing becomes until you stop altogether. It's worse when you've consumed both alcohol and heroin, as alcohol works to repress the excitatory signals that tell you to keep breathing. Most of the time, the pulse is not affected and if you give an overdose victim an opiate blocker or even mouth-to-mouth until their lungs start again, they'll snap out of it.

None of this helped Ardian. He was drunk and doped, with a bronchial infection left over from pneumonia, which he'd contracted before he was fired from the care facility and had been fighting since. His lungs, weighed down by the overdose, couldn't clear the fluid building up in them. He drowned in his own vomit, alone.

He was long gone by the time his housemates woke up to find him, lying dead on the couch. One of them called the ambulance service, who called the cops, who told us. I got on the phone and started calling around with the news and slowly the house filled up with mourners. Friends and relatives came in weeping, or silent, or they stood around awkwardly, making sympathetic noises.

People kept offering me cigarettes. I didn't want them but I took them and puffed them down anyway. It seemed appropriate somehow, in the weird, stilted half-world I found myself in suddenly – something to keep my hands busy. I needed a job to do.

And I had a job to do. Someone had to identify the body. Still in shock, my folks and I left the party, climbed into the Pintara station wagon and drove to the morgue. We filled out a couple of forms and stood around. I remember everything being grey, the washed-out colour of concrete after rain.

They walked us into a viewing room, a tiny adjunct with a big glass window in it. On the other side of the window, Ardian was lying on a steel examination table. My parents went up to the window, holding hands. That detail stuck with me. They weren't terribly affectionate and they didn't hold hands often.

'Yes,' Mum said, her face crinkling, 'that's him.' She turned away sobbing, and Dad led her back into the other room. I went up and pressed my nose against the glass.

There are a lot of writers who try to dress up death in pretty words to make it more palatable, but I can't do that. Death looks like what it is, and Ardian looked dead. I could see where he'd bled, trickles had dried on the side of his face from his nose and mouth, two rivulets that merged in a fork that ran down his cheek, black blood on blue skin. His skin was starved of oxygen, a choked-off purple-blue that whitened as it moved down his body. I could see every bit of sparse chest hair, every follicle of his beard, or at least as much of a beard as he could grow. He was twenty-one.

I turned away from the window, and we went home.

We held the funeral at a Buddhist temple in Springvale. Hamish and I helped carry the coffin and, as we loaded it into the hearse, my little brother burst into tears. I didn't really know what to say so I just kind of shook him by the shoulder, feeling completely out of my depth.

I'd just given the eulogy. The night before I'd sat staring at the cursor blinking against the screen. What could I write? What could I possibly say when nothing would ever be right again in a future that stretched out forever, barren and empty?

At the wake, held in our backyard, I got quietly drunk and tried to stay away from the hippies. Ardian had been fond of ConFest, a bi-annual alternative lifestyle festival, or, as one jaded attendee described it to me, 'A bunch of old hippies who have tricked you into paying a hundred bucks to show you their penis,' and the backyard was filling up with alternative lifestylers. For every old friend of Ardian's who came up to me and collapsed wailing in my arms, I would get some dreadlocked neophyte who would sidle up and stroke my shoulder with a sweaty palm, murmuring, 'Your brother had, like, a really special aura.'

I'd decamped to the pavement out the front of my house, leaning with my back against the fence. I had a beer and some kind of cake, but I couldn't eat so I broke up the slice and threw the pieces to some seagulls that had gathered around. I was so absorbed in watching them fight over the crumbs, I didn't notice the hippie appear next to me, in a flurry of bangles and flowing skirts.

'You like birds, huh?'

'I guess.'

'Ardian liked birds.'

'I don't think we ever talked about birds,' I said.

'He liked all living things.' She nodded and smiled, agreeing with the thing she had just said, and then took my hand. 'Can I tell you something? This morning, I was sad about the funeral but then, when I was sitting meditating on Ardian's spirit, a sparrow came up and landed on my windowsill, and I knew that was Ardian's soul visiting me with a message.' The flower child paused and looked deep into my eyes. 'I hope that makes you feel better.' She finished by smiling at me and squeezing my knee reassuringly, and all at once I was angrier than I'd ever been.

'He's dead!' I hissed. 'You daft fucking hippie! What do you think is happening? That he died so he could come back as a bird? That instead of travelling the cosmos or reincarnating or whatever the fuck, he became a fucking *sparrow* so he could visit *you*, and let you know that tie-dye is a good choice for you? Go fuck yourself,' I shrieked, and stormed past her and back into the wake, shaking with rage.

My dad came up to me. 'You look angry,' he said.

'Yep.'

'I'm angry too,' he said. 'What the fuck was he thinking?' And we stood, being angry in a room full of sad people.

There was plenty to be angry about. A few days after the funeral, Dad, Hamish and I headed out to clean up Ardian's house. When we'd identified the body the mortician had given me Ardian's wallet, which was in his pocket when he died. Inside it was a one-dollar coin and a necklace he used to wear fastened with sticky tape: those were the only things he owned that couldn't have been traded for smack. In his house all his CDs and musical instruments had disappeared.

A stained mattress lay bare on the floor, with a pile of clothes and blankets strewn across it. I stared at it for a minute, and an image of Ardian coughing and spluttering his last came to me. I turned away and made myself busy.

Apart from the mattress the only furniture was a coffee table covered in old mugs, and milk crates and cardboard boxes full with his possessions. He'd never unpacked. We browsed through his books and magazines, sorting those we would keep into boxes, those we would discard into bin bags. I found a copy of *The Great Gatsby* and sat for a moment holding it. He'd told me a couple of weeks earlier that he'd finally read the book and was going to throw a mint julep party to celebrate. Up on his wall, on a little shelf built into the alcove, stood half a bottle of whisky and an untouched bottle of crème de menthe. I guessed he'd never had that party. The bottles went into the bin bag.

It didn't take long to pack up Ardian's belongings. I took the books and clothes; Hamish took his magazines and VHS tapes. My dad took a few keepsakes, school IDs, a box of love letters, those worthless sentimental things you cart from house to house but never look at, content just to keep them safe until you grow older and take them out to find they've appreciated through the years. We left the mattress for the next punter.

A week after the funeral, one of Ardian's friends came around to give us some videotapes of a holiday to New South Wales he'd taken a year earlier. The tape opened with Ardian and his friend talking shit in a hotel room, and then cut to a series of adventures around Sydney. We saw him chatting up some girls, walking across a fence like a tightrope, playing hacky sack, smoking a joint on the seawall of Circular Quay. He wandered the streets of Kings Cross looking for a light and finally asked a bemused welder to spark his cigarette with a blowtorch. It was funny; we were all surprised by how little it hurt. Then it hurt a lot. 'Oh, God, I need a joint,' declared Dad. He hit pause and went to the kitchen to roll one, leaving Ardian frozen on the screen, smiling at something over the camerawoman's shoulder that only he could see.

The dead are not static. Long after they are gone, your relationship with them remains, grinding on, as relentless and world-changing as tectonic plates. Every night for months, I would dream about Ardian suddenly walking through the door, or picking me up from school, or calling me on the phone, with some simple explanation for how his death was a mistake, that everyone could stop worrying, that he'd been living on an island in the Philippines, that he was fine. 'Of course I didn't die of a *heroin overdose*,' he told me in one dream. 'As if. What a cliché!'

The turning points in life, the really important decisions, are rarely dramatic. The first time someone tries heroin isn't life-altering, but the three-hundredth time, the time their heart stops, sure is. Every human is an unwieldy vessel, weighed down with hopes and dreams. We turn so slowly that we don't even realise we are moving at all. We creatures of habit, our momentum is all-consuming. For every action there are consequences we could never anticipate; it's how we grow, each of us, from worms into butterflies, flapping our wings and making tornadoes on the other side of the world.

Nearly half a century after Cliff Ross hit on the idea of feeding birds to drum up business for Fantasyland, every day at 8.45 a.m. someone will still turn up to feed the pelicans who gather on the foreshore. It's something of an institution. Tourists driving up the coast will detour through Kalbarri to see the majestic birds glide in for food. They are disappointed on days when nobody turns up to feed the pelicans, but not as much as the birds themselves, who, if they aren't fed on time, will waddle across the road to the museum, pecking on the door, impatient for the long-dead Ross to come out and give them their fish.

IO

People have a habit of burying grief in metaphor – black dogs, roller-coasters, labyrinths, fog monsters – all in an effort to make real the suffocating bleakness that descends over them. They tend to glorify the concept, to try to turn it into something epic: a creature to be overcome, a journey that starts with a step. So here's my metaphor: grief is a long, dark night in a wet sleeping bag at a shitty music festival that everyone seems to be enjoying but you. It's cold, it's raining, it's unpleasant, but you're not going to wriggle out of your damp cocoon because the alternatives are even worse.

Our family was broken, and everything we encountered fed

back into what we'd lost. Our thoughts were circular, a macabre game of Six Degrees where you could bring any moment back to your unhappiness in a few easy steps.

'Where are you going, Liam?'

'To Ben's house.'

'What are you going to do there?'

'Hang out.'

'Are you going to do drugs?'

'No, just play Nintendo.'

'Your brother played Nintendo, and then he did drugs. And now he's dead.'

You'd think that when drugs start killing your family you would shy away from them, maybe rethink your lifestyle choices: take up squash or macramé or something. But that's not how it happened for us. Instead, we kept taking the drugs but we turned up the volume, thinking they'd give us comfort, some respite from the grief. Humans are simple creatures: we'll lean towards something that we once enjoyed long after it's no longer pleasurable, long after it's no longer an effective crutch.

The main problem with medicating your grief with drugs is that it doesn't help. It only seems to, and even then only for an hour. The high is familiar and therefore comforting, but what it does to your brain doesn't help. You're still sad and now you're also anxious and depressed, your brain chemistry all in a lather. You'll spend the time that you're stoned, the hours, the days, the years, pushing your memories and feelings around like a toddler with vegetables on a plate. In the end, your mind will look chewed over, but you won't have digested anything. The grief builds and builds and you never get better. You just get sadder and sadder until, one day, you decide to die.

It was the morning of a school day, probably a Wednesday because that was the day I'd wag phys ed to drink wine in the garage, and I'd gone into the laundry to look for my sports uniform, which I needed in order to sneak out of school without getting busted. Hungover and cranky, I stumbled from the laundry to the kitchen, which was empty. This was unusual – normally this time of morning Mum would be in the kitchen, having a quiet cry into the juicer. From outside I could hear muffled wailing, so I made myself a bowl of Weet-Bix, which I ate as I sauntered outside to find Dad's suicide machine.

When we first left Labassa and my parents were fighting all the time, they would often end an argument by yelling, 'Well, then, I'm going to fucking kill myself!' before storming out of the room. They talked about suicide with the sort of enthusiasm that left me unable to wait to try it. I didn't really understand what it meant to kill oneself, but I could tell that it was very exciting.

When the fighting got bad I would retreat to the end of the backyard to play with my Teenage Mutant Ninja Turtle dolls while waiting for the quarrel to end. 'I'm going to fucking kill myself,' Splinter would tell Leonardo, in my growly, slightly racist Splinter voice. 'If it wasn't for you and your brothers I would have defeated Shredder and the Technodrome years ago and I would be happy.' Then I would have the turtles kill themselves one by one – Donatello built a eutha-nasia machine, Leonardo fell on his sword – and Splinter was happy again.

My games with the Ninja Turtles would escalate until I climbed onto the back of the couch and threw myself off, emulating Gollum at the end of *The Lord of the Rings*. I used to follow Dad around the house while he was trying to practise guitar and beg him to help me kill myself, as I understood it from cartoons: buy me some dynamite, drop an anvil on my head. Dad tried his best to turn my imagination in a more wholesome direction.

He would often read books to me. My favourite was a French children's book, *The House that Beebo Built*, which we read cover to cover every night before bed. It was about a Parisian Metro worker and inventor who retires to the countryside to build his dream house, which he packs with all kinds of weird inventions. Eventually some evil property developers come to tear down his house so he locks all the doors and starts building a tower annex to get away from them. When he runs out of building materials, he uses four planks of wood to build a staircase, taking the plank from the bottom to fashion the next step, with nothing but faith, ingenuity and a touch of po-mo to escape into the clouds.

Dad's suicide machine wasn't Beebo's work. It wasn't even Philip Nitschke's. It was a bit like the playful death machines I'd built for Donatello when I would play suicides with my Ninja Turtle action figures: amateurish and improvised. Dad had taken the family sta-tion wagon and used a roll of electrical tape and the garden hose to connect the exhaust pipe to the driver's-side window. The window was sealed with tape to create a vacuum and he was sitting behind the wheel, revving the engine. It was the same car that Ardian had learned to drive in, the same hose that had grown incrementally shorter every time he'd cut a length off to make a bong out of a Gatorade bottle. It was lazy symbolism.

It took me a minute to figure out what was happening. I had the vague impression that Mum was screaming and Hamish was crying, but everything else was fuzzy. I'd like to say that I assumed that special kind of cool reserved for action heroes, where they instinctively know what to do, but, given that this was 2001, it's safe to say I was probably already high.

First I walked around to the driver's-side window and tapped on it. Dad ignored me, kept his eyes closed and revved the engine again. The Nissan screamed to be let out of neutral. I tried talking to him, then to punch in the window, which isn't as easy as it looks in the movies. My fist bounced off the glass, making me feel silly on top of everything else. Sucking on my bruised knuckles, I walked to the back of the car where I tugged the hose out of the exhaust. A great cloud of sooty gas choked out. I walked to the front of the car and tapped on the windscreen, this time with the hose, until Dad looked up. He slumped in his seat and stopped revving. Then he turned off the ignition and sat quietly until it was time for him to go to work.

I was cross at Dad for making me hurt my knuckles but part of me admired him. He'd had the balls to make a move towards the checkout, albeit in a melodramatic, baby-boomerish sort of way, and it seemed like a sensible option. All of us, I think, thought about it.

Throughout 2001 I did my best to kill myself too, without ever really thinking about it. I'd inherited Ardian's motorcycle and I would ride it around, drunk and high, without a helmet, impressed at how cavalier I was. Occasionally, just occasionally, I'd get a sudden urge to oversteer into approaching traffic. It was a flash: a searing, visceral, almost uncontrollable desire to bang on the throttle and drop into the road, so real that I could feel myself sliding and crunching under the oncoming wheel, the adrenaline, the pain, the blackness to follow. But it passed as quickly as it came.

The term 'death wish' is a misnomer. As I experienced it, it was more an ambivalence to the idea of dying: a Zen-like acceptance that death will come soon and be welcomed with the stoic resignation of an English bedmate. It was being so high and so low at the same time, a sensation of being pushed up and pulled down so that I hung suspended in a sparkling amniotic numbness. It was the moment I came off my motorbike and lay bruised with the cold night air coming in through the helmet's cracked visor, realising I had nearly died, and not minding.

About halfway through Year 12, I woke up in the middle of the night after dreaming of Ardian giving me a pep talk on the merits of death.

'It's great!' he said. 'No hangovers, no need for money. And I'm not saying there's a heaven but the women over here!' He made an appreciative lip-smacking noise, and I started awake, drenched in sweat and suddenly resolute. I looked around my room, counting out the contents of my pill bottles, the little pharmacy that kept me upright, calculating how much Valium and codeine I had, the tricky chemistry they could unleash in my system. I folded out my flick-knife and tested its bald point against a finger. Down the road, I recalled, not across the street.

I felt I should call somebody and let them know what was happening. After my first few calls rang out, I called up my friend Ponchik, the one person trashy enough to be awake at that hour. I told him I was feeling low, that I was thinking of ending it. He thought for a moment, then said, 'Liam, I owe you six hundred bucks. If you kill yourself, you're never going to see that again. Are you sure you want that?'

'No.'

'Then don't.'

So I didn't kill myself, and Ponchik still owes me $600.

The spectre was there for all of us. Even now, even after all these years, my heart still lurches whenever anyone in my family phones, and my thumb pauses before I can make it slide across the screen to pick up the call. In those few seconds, my mind stalls as I calculate the possibilities, going over the events of the previous weeks like a card counter, trying to predict what grim news I'll hear on picking up. I see my little brother beaten to death by a meth head after a drug deal gone wrong. I'm caught in the visceral stillness of it – I feel the crunch of baseball bat on soft flesh and brittle bone.

Or maybe it's Dad. Has he swerved his motorcycle into the wrong lane of the highway that takes him home? Or maybe it's Mum, and it'll be the slow-burn cancer, of the lung or the stomach or the brain, and the years or months or days ticking down to a frail, whimpered exit.

But these are just moments. You can't cruise forever in the wake of a tragedy, any more than you can mend a broken heart by hitching it to someone else's happiness. We die alone, yes, but we are born alone too, so the people who enrich our lives are gifts, whether they are here for a lifetime or just a few moments. The trick is not to forget that. Whenever I'm at my darkest, I remember that there is goodness in the world. That there is pain and hardship and foolishness and misery, but that is what it is to be human. Now, whenever I get down, I remember that my life will pass in an instant, and I remember the value of the sacred, transient miracle of the heart beating in my chest, each moment impossibly precious, and that today, maybe today, Ponchik will pay me back my $600.

11

Our house, which had always been too small for the three of us young men, seemed suddenly cavernous. With the blinds drawn I could wander through the gloom and not encounter anyone, just hear different pitches of weeping seep in from far-flung parts of the house like some ill-conceived piece of performance art. We all became familiar with the cadences of misery – stifled before-school sobbing, the slow, steady drip of tears down a nose onto a dinner plate, the uncorked animal bellow of a grieving father in the shower after the workday. Pictures of Ardian covered every available surface. The decorative bongs he had crafted in Year 8 ceramics class, which until now had been hidden from guests behind bookshelves, became priceless talismans, displayed prominently throughout the house.

The sadness was insidious. If you luxuriate long enough in your misery, then that misery becomes a luxury. For one thing, it gave us carte blanche to do all the drugs we could get our hands on. Mum and Dad smoked a lot of pot in the weeks after Ardian's death, sitting in silence at the kitchen table, lighting the next joint from the last, the only sounds the crackle of tobacco and the pop of a stray seed.

I dealt with it in my own way. Since being at home got me down, after a couple of weeks off for mourning, I went back to work, throwing myself at it with a grim verve. Like unhappy people since the dawn of time, I found I could ignore the dense weight of my heart by focusing on things I could quantify. Buy this much product; sell this much; make these margins. I didn't love maths but numbers always did what I told them, and that was infinitely comforting when all else was cockeyed.

Part of me, a large part, ever-expanding, loved my work. Being out of the house, driving through Melbourne every night, and the little adrenaline rush when I was in a scuffle, or a police cruiser drove by in the opposite direction to Sunny's car, took my mind off my problems.

The parties were great as well. In a town like Melbourne, even in the sleepy south-east, an intricate web of scenes and socioeconomic strata weaved their invisible threads through the streets. Crack the surface of the suburbs and underneath there's an ecosystem of subcultures desperately trying to thrive. They could be wildly different, but, in my experience, they all had one thing in common: everybody wanted to get high.

Of a weekend I might make house calls to a dozen parties, whose attendees ranged from twitchy covens of gamers who lugged hulking desktop computers around to each other's houses for days-long *Counter-Strike* tournaments that ran on weed and pizza, to jumping frat-style parties. The most lucrative were thrown by the private-school kids in the area, where students could afford to spend money and time taking drugs. My most valuable clients over the years were elite fuck-ups whose teachers looked the other way when they cheated on their VCE exams in the later years of high school.

It was at a party like that where I met Sarah, who for a couple of years helped me to forget that I was miserable. The chronology of most of my formative memories is a bit unmoored in my poor old brain but I can date this meeting to around 2001 because Sisqó's 'Thong Song' was playing when I first saw her. The crowd was typical of that time and place: Polish-Jewish schoolgirls, surly Russian homeboys, Italian girls who came to get buzzed on Bacardi Breezers and give the unsmiling homeboys hand jobs beneath their FUBU jackets.

I'd turned up with a couple of friends who knew someone who knew someone who wanted to buy a bag. Once we'd sold it, we hung about, stealing beers from the bathtub and trying to chat up a group of girls, one of whom was Sarah: a cute, fresh-faced high-school student with a nice smile who seemed to buy whatever far-fetched horseshit I was trying to sell her – I think I was trying to impress her by name-dropping the Cat Empire.

Before we left, Sarah swooped in, flowing hippie skirt swirling, bracelets jangling, flushed from the dance floor, tipsy and giddy, to ask if I wanted her number.

'Give me a call!' she giggled. 'All the other girls will freak out about your gross *goy* dick! Go out with me!' What could I be but charmed?

I called Sarah the next day. She didn't remember me but agreed to go on a date. I suspect she only said she'd go out with me because it would piss off her mum.

Sarah was sweet-natured, and I was shocked to find out she didn't do drugs at all. She hardly even drank – I'd caught her on a rare night. I found the concept strange; I'd never really been close to someone who was sober. It weirded me out that she could live her life without ever getting drunk or high. She was a couple of inches shorter than me, which is uncommon, fine-featured and beautiful. She wore her hair long, twisted into tight braids that were close enough to dread-locks to remind me soothingly of my hippie roots but weren't festy and gross like the real things.

The only flaws I could find with Sarah were her obnoxious rat-like dogs, her elder sister's unwavering hostility towards me and the fact that she was theatrically crazy. She had dreams of becoming a fine artist who was driven by her demons – a kosher Jean-Michel Basquiat – and so when she was diagnosed with an anxiety disorder, she put up her mainsail and went with it.

She had panic attacks at school, at work, at the DVD store when I wanted to rent something other than a Leonardo DiCaprio film. Whenever we had an argument she would get a few minutes in before hyperventilating and screaming. 'I'm having an attack,' she would wail, 'I can't feel my face!' until I went down the road to pick up some takeaway lasagne. As it turns out, she would grow up to be a hell of an artist, but only once she stopped trying to be so tortured.

There were other problems too, such as the fact we couldn't understand a fucking thing about each other. Her friends baffled me. They were lovely and welcoming enough towards me, but we didn't have a lot of common ground. Like me, most of them were raised in mansions, but they got to keep theirs. They were born to palatial houses in Caulfield and, apart from a couple who burned out in India or moved to Israel, they all ended up marrying people they went to high school with and bought houses one suburb away from their parents. Of course that happens to kids at other Australian high schools; I suppose I just noticed it more as an outsider to the Jewish community. Even though I tried my hardest, I would always be on the periphery. I tried so hard to fit in – wearing Diesel, learning how to swear in Hebrew – that I went a little too far and ended up spouting Yiddish truisms like some suburban Woody Allen. In the end, Sarah had to take me aside to ask me not to sing any more songs from *Fiddler on the Roof*. 'A little matzo ball–fever is okay, but people will start to think that you're anti-Semitic.'

Sarah and her friends were an extremely tight-knit group. They'd known each other since birth and it was understood that their own kids would grow up together, and they had a sense of community responsibility that came with that. My own moral compass had been forged out of a blend of Catholic guilt and escapist hippie opportunism, so we were coming at life from different angles. I was thrown by their civic-mindedness so I can only imagine what they thought of me. Often, I felt I confused them. I assumed at the time that, sheltered as they were, they'd never really got to know a *goy* before, although looking back, there may have been other confounding factors about me.

I didn't shy away from the fact that I sold drugs for a living. I told anyone who would listen, taking on clients I should have run shrieking from at first sight: strung-out meth heads who wanted weed to come down and scummy part-time tradies who did burglaries and invited me to 'go the pros' with them. I became lazy and sloppy. If a client lived nearby, I would call a driver or walk out to meet them on a street corner, but otherwise I would have them pull up in front of the house and drive me around the block while we negotiated. Sarah wasn't exactly happy that I spent so much time around drugs, but, for me, the money was good and I was trying my best to keep up with her clique.

While Sarah lived humbly compared to some of her friends, the wealth being effortlessly kicked around in her social circle astounded me. I'd been raised to believe that eating out in a restaurant was a luxury reserved for special occasions: weddings or maybe birthdays. I remember my godparents taking me out to a yum cha restaurant for my seventh birthday and being exposed to such a vast expansion of the world of consumption that I stood at the threshold hyperventilating like Bad Boy Bubby when he first leaves the house. So whenever Sarah's crowd would ask me to go out for lunch, it freaked me out. They had allowances, bar- and bat-mitzvah windfalls, trust funds. None of them had to work after-school jobs. When they finished school for the day they took the tram down Glenhuntly Road and sat in cafés, lingering over hot chocolates and gossip.

I should stress that all these Jewish-Australian princesses and princelings were lovely. Even though I was an uppity pissant of dubious moral hygiene, they went out of their way to invite me to their holiday houses to go dirt-biking or boating, or to take me as a date to Sarah's debutante ball, which, being *goy*, I couldn't attend as an escort. But I felt clumsy and inadequate, unable to handle money gracefully like people born into it instinctively can. My instinct is to take every dollar I get to a hiding spot under a bridge and to hiss at anyone who comes near – although that compulsion is not quite as strong as my in-built Celtic urge to blow the whole lot on ostentatious drinking binges.

Before drug money came into my life, taking a girl out to dinner would have sent me spiralling into my own face-numbing panic attack, but I came to learn how to splash money around. I had started to covet nice cars, to see the appeal of investing in coal. I became good friends with Ponchik, who looked and acted like a Stalinist propaganda cartoon of a Jewish capitalist. He was a music producer and entrepreneur, and was forever starting businesses, making a fortune and then blowing it all on drugs and strippers. He was charming, ruthless, effortlessly winning – a sociopathic whirlwind of money and greed and fun. We would smoke joints in his car, listening to Tricky while he would rattle off his latest evil scheme.

Together we mortgaged the last few months of our last year at school. When our final exams rolled around, I performed miserably. I had expected that I would, but I was still surprised at just how badly I did. Not as surprised as my parents, who were crushed with disappointment at my mediocre results, and who screamed at me until I fled the house to eat pills with Ponchik. He'd never had the same drama. For his final exams he stashed all the answers in the bathroom of the hall before the test and slipped out halfway through to get high and finish his papers off the cheat-sheets. He did well, that Ponchik.

One night he mentioned, with the casual lilt that suggested he'd carefully crafted the idea to appear spontaneous and would not take no for an answer, that a friend of his had some cocaine. 'It's a bargain,' he said. 'Three hundred dollars.' I told him that $300 sounded like a lot of money. He told me that $300 was only a lot of money to people who thought that it sounded like a lot of money. He had a kind of circular logic that was as dangerous as it was infectious. 'Once you change your mindset and stop worrying about money, then money will stop worrying about you.' Everything he said sounded like a self-help truism and, as he passed me a joint, this seemed to make perfect sense. We argued for a while, but, with some help from Ponchik, curiosity finally beat down the Catholic grandmother in me, and we drove off to score some coke. A few of us chipped in fifties and we crowded into the back seat of Ponchik's dad's Volvo as a dealer jumped in the front, made the exchange and then vanished into the night.

We drove back to Marco's house, piled out of the car and rushed upstairs. The atmosphere was festive. As Ponchik unwrapped the little parcel of tinfoil, it could have been Christmas, were fewer of us Jewish. He opened the wrap and tapped out the contents onto a CD case with a flourish, and showed us how to roll up a note and snort a line. He repeated it with the other nostril, and then snorted a few more lines for good measure. By the time he got around to passing over the CD, most of the gram was gone, and we were grumbling.

It got passed around to a couple of people before it was dropped into my lap. I jammed the note up a nostril, then bent down to snort the line. I'd seen it done in movies, the snorting of the line, the theatrical gasping and eye watering. This was much simpler: the coke inhaled easily, bled into my nasal cavity and began its tireless tramp towards my brain. It didn't hurt at all. In fact, it felt great. I felt great.

The first sharp jolt receded as a pleasant, cool numbness enveloped my nose and spread across the rest of my face. It felt a little uncomfortable and I was having trouble swallowing, but luckily my speech didn't seem to be affected. The best thing about cocaine is the way it short circuits your brain and shuts down reticence, humility and basic human decency, in favour of a spiking heart rate and an urgent need to editorialise.

Usually, whenever my friends were bantering, I was always lagging behind, trying to craft the perfect line, a joke I could lob into the conversation like an urbane smart bomb. Now gags and cutting observations exploded in glorious starbursts that came rushing out of my mouth faster than I could properly articulate them. Thanks, cocaine!

Soon I was sweating and my jaw hurt from flapping, but I hadn't felt this good in years. I wiped the sweat from my hands onto my jeans, and then kept rubbing my thighs feverishly, suddenly aware of the tactile wonderlands that were the muscles in my legs. My whole body shivered with glorious pleasure, every drag on a cigarette was at once soothing and exciting, and everything I said seemed brilliant, an endless cascade of wit that poured out of me. I reached for another line.

Later, at home, I lay in bed, my heart rattling my ribcage. I was afraid to sleep, convinced that if I closed my eyes, I would drift off and never wake up. I thought sadly of my parents finding me in the morning, cold and grey, stretched out on my futon. A great iceberg of anxiety shuddered through my chest and an inexplicable sorrow settled over me. Although I'd smoked a bit of pot when I was younger and taken the occasional pill, I'd never snorted anything before.

I didn't know Ardian had done heroin until after his death. That was a foreign world to me, one I'd never had an interest in. In my mind, drugs could be divided into a neat binary: heroin, coke, all the powdered drugs that came in sinister little bags, and then everything else. The two or three lines of coke I'd done that night felt like a transgression: I'd dipped into something grown-up and wrong, and I'd get my comeuppance. I lay paralysed by grief, for my imminent death, for my parents, for my surviving brother, for the years I wouldn't have.

Eventually, I closed my eyes and when I opened them again it was the morning, and my mum was hurrying me to get ready for school. I hadn't been dying; I was just coming down. All I needed to do was another bump, and then another half an hour after that, and to just keep doing that every day until I graduated high school, then, for a lark, the next decade. Live and learn.

12

Sarah and I had been going out for more than a year, but there were a hundred reasons why I was reluctant to introduce her mum to my folks, not least matters of class, religion and taste. Sarah had been pushing the idea for ages, though, and after a while I acquiesced. I was still anxious about it and so contrived to make it as casual a meet-and-greet as possible. On school nights Sarah usually came around to my place for a couple of hours. If her mum came to pick her up, that would be a good time to introduce her to my parents. There would be a quick doorstop chat, or, at worst, a cup of coffee in a kitchen that had been carefully cleaned and aired out so as not to be incriminating.

At 10.30 one night, Mrs Lubow parked out the front of our house and knocked on the door. I ushered her into the hallway, where my parents stood freshly scrubbed and clear-eyed, and there was a round of handshaking and awkward smiling. Dad cracked a dad joke and Mrs Lubow nodded politely. For a couple of minutes I thought that maybe the whole thing wouldn't be as difficult as I'd feared. I was congratulating myself on orchestrating the perfect rendez-vous and thinking that perhaps I could leverage my new-found diplomatic nous into a high-powered career in the foreign service, when the police raided.

The cops had been watching the house for some time and decided to make their move that particular night. Earlier in the even-ing, my buddy Dave had come by to score a bag. I'd known him for ages – we'd been good friends in school and sometimes we'd skip class to smoke weed and eat chips. Now that we'd graduated from high school, he was spending the summer in much the same way, stoking his prodigious appetite by smoking bushels of weed. A few hours before Sarah's mum was due, he'd made small talk with Sarah while I measured out his purchase, and then he waddled out the front to his parents' Ford Festiva to head home. The unmarked car that had been watching my house peeled off to follow him before pulling him over a few streets away. The cops then dragged him in for questioning.

Dave was an ideal criminal informant, in that he was a craven piece of shit with the ability to sign his own name. The boy was never destined for great things, being unwieldy, pale and easily scared. He was full of insecurities, as though he were being operated by a dozen fearful little men inside a sweaty, meaty sack. When the police brought him in he heartily affirmed whatever crimes they suggested I had committed or would go on to commit. By the time Dave signed off on the confessional statement, which stopped just short of accusing me of witchcraft, the police were under the impression that I was far more dangerous and competent a criminal than the reality. They returned to my house in greater numbers, and better armed than they needed to be, strictly speaking.

Toting a warrant and a disproportionate sense of my importance, officers in unmarked cars had been watching the house, waiting. They were hoping to catch me in the act of selling drugs, before swooping in and busting me. When Mrs Lubow pulled up out the front of the house in her nicely appointed coupé, the surveillance team decided that she must be my dealer.

A heavy-set man in a polo shirt advanced up the driveway. I saw him coming and left my parents and Mrs Lubow making chitchat to meet him. Despite my best efforts, I'd occasionally get walk-ins – those out of phone credit or just too obtuse to take instruction – looking to score.

'Can I help you?' I asked.

'Are you Liam Pieper?'

'Yes, I am, but . . . this isn't a good time.'

'No,' he agreed. 'It isn't.'

Just before he grabbed me, I caught a flash of the Lacoste logo on his shirt and my heart sank. I'm not sure when or why the undercover officers of the world decided that the mid-tier designer polo was the cloak of urban invisibility, but every time a cop has sprung out of the shadows at me, it's always been there, faithful as a hound, that fucking crocodile.

Poor Mrs Lubow. She was just being polite, going through the motions of making nice with my parents, passing the time until Sarah dumped me and married a doctor. She wasn't expecting this. One minute it was all, 'Isn't it unseasonably cold?' and the next it was, 'Where's the dope, bitch?' The police, after charging her down, realised that this forty-something divorcee wasn't the drug lord they'd been angling for. Disappointed, they let her go. I don't know who was more surprised: Mrs Lubow, who found herself suddenly being given a pat down by armed cops, or the officers themselves, who dumped out her purse expecting bags of pills only to find travel packs of sugar-free sweetener. Mrs Lubow gathered up Sarah and stormed out as I stood staring forlornly after them. This was going to be hard to explain.

Being raided is always awful – for obvious reasons if you're a criminal and your house is packed full of contraband, but it's just as bad if the cops have it wrong. As long as they have a warrant, they're going to wreck the place. Years ago, some friends of the family were running a candle workshop out of their suburban kitchen. Somehow the cops had been tipped off that their art collective was a front for a meth lab, and an armed biohazard team stormed the place to find incriminating-looking saucepans of boiling paraffin wax everywhere. The older cops realised what was happening pretty quickly, but the younger ones stubbornly arrested everyone and carted off a ton of wax for analysis. In the process they trashed the place, tearing apart books and pulling the stuffing out of sofas and soft toys. That one never even made it to court, but you can't blame the kids for being methodical.

My cops were also methodical. A bored-looking police photographer opened each drawer of my desk and snapped it, before Lacoste guy yanked them all out and spilled the contents over my futon. If Lacoste found something of interest, he bagged it, tagged it and had it photographed. Otherwise, it went into the growing pile of discarded junk on the futon.

The first drawer was fine: textbooks and homework left over from school, a few notebooks filled with terrible poetry. The second was dicier: more notebooks, but one with a ledger of my customers and details of the money they owed me. I had the name written in Korean script, but the numbers were laid out in neat Arabic numerals. Lacoste, already bored with the notebooks – thank God for the human instinct to flinch from embarrassing poetry – flicked through the ledger.

'What the fuck is this?'

'It's my homework.'

'Why's it in Chinese?'

'It's Korean.'

'You speak Korean?'

'Not well.'

'Why are the numbers in English?'

'Those are translations.'

Lacoste shrugged, and tossed it onto the rubbish pile.

The third drawer down was trouble. It was where I stored everything I didn't want my mum to find, fastened with a flimsy IKEA lock. Inside I had a fistful of cash in twenties and fifties, along with a few grams of weed stored in individual foil packages. On their own, either of these things would have been damning, but it was stupid of me to store them together. The cops told me as much as they tagged them as evidence.

They bagged up each item in separate envelopes before picking through the rest of the drawer. Then Lacoste found *Bondage Fairies*.

Bondage Fairies was a manga comic, a kind of high-kink hentai *Captain Planet*, in which two fairies living in a fantastical forest battle the forces of evil while teaching readers about the environment and sexuality. My friend Herchal, who knew I liked manga, had brought it back from Japan for my eighteenth birthday as a joke, and I'd completely forgotten about it. In this particular issue, the protagonist, Pfil, saves the day by magically growing a giant dick and using it to fuck a goblin to death when he threatens the biodiversity of an old-growth forest.

Lacoste was a grizzled cop. Pushing forty, muscular, professionally expressionless. When he spoke it was in clipped, efficient sentences, evenly modulated, giving nothing away beyond that he was bored. As he flicked through *Bondage Fairies*, though, his eyes widened and he let out a long, disapproving, 'Jesus.' The other cops crowded around to read over his shoulder.

'I think,' said one, 'that we've got a sex pervert on our hands.'

'I'm not, honestly,' I protested weakly. 'It was a gift from my friend Herchal.'

'Well, don't worry. There'll be plenty of gifts from friends like "Herchal" where you're going.'

Then they found my ponytail. Until very recently I'd worn my hair in a long, wavy cascade down my back. In my mind I looked like a Red Hot Chili Pepper, whose records I listened to relentlessly, but looking back at photos of the era, I can see the effect was more juvenile sex offender than Anthony Kiedis. A year or so back, Lilly had talked me into cutting it off. We threw a party, got drunk and she bundled my hair together with one of her hair ties and cut off everything above the knot with a pair of kitchen shears. Then a few of us joked around with the severed ponytail for a while before I absentmindedly chucked it into the bottom drawer of my desk and promptly forgot about it, until now as Lacoste retrieved it gingerly. He didn't even speak, just looked at me with a mixture of curiosity and disgust.

'Whose hair is this?'

'It's my hair.'

'Why do you have it?'

'I don't know,' I answered honestly.

'Is it a sex thing?'

'No.' This threw me. That interpretation hadn't occurred to me. 'Is there a ponytail sex thing?'

He tossed the ponytail into the junk pile, and gave me a look that said, *You tell me, Bondage Fairy*.

Once they had piled all my possessions together on my futon, they reached down and flipped over the mattress. Through the slats of the bed, nestled among the dust bunnies, could be seen the package of Glucodin energy powder I used to cut my cocaine. It was roughly the same weight and consistency as coke, and, importantly, it was tasteless: an ideal neutral substance to use as cutter. When the cops saw it, they got very excited.

Lacoste picked up the box and dipped a finger into it. He tasted it and then asked me what it was.

'That's energy powder,' I said. It crossed my mind that 'energy powder' sounded an awful lot like slang for crystal meth. But, then again, so do most things.

'What do you use it for?'

'I put it on my breakfast cereal.'

'Why is it under your bed?'

'I like to have breakfast in bed,' I said, inspired.

'So you put it on your cereal? You don't use speed or coke?'

'Are you crazy? Do you know how much that would cost? I don't know how much you guys make but I don't have that kind of money.'

They boxed it up and took it as evidence anyway.

Once they were done turning the house upside down, the cops carried the boxes of evidence out to the cars. I sat on the stoop and fretted. My first jolt of adrenaline was fading and I was starting to think more clearly, which wasn't calming. Any way I quantified it, I was in deep trouble. They had been thorough in collecting every bit of evidence against me but I'd had two pieces of luck: firstly, they hadn't seized my ledger; and, secondly, in confusing a middle-aged homemaker for a drug lord, they'd neglected to search my person. In my pocket, next to a packet of Dunhills, my mobile phone was loaded with incriminating numbers and text messages. I had to find some way to lose that before I was processed. I looked across to the cop charged with keeping an eye on me. He shifted to meet my eyes.

'Do you mind if I have a cigarette?' I asked him.

'I don't care. Got one for me?'

I tapped out a Dunhill for each of us. 'Do you have a light?'

He nodded and produced a lighter. He lit mine first, then his. While the cop was lighting his, figuring his night vision would be thrown by the flame, I pulled out my phone and tossed it behind me so that it landed in the long grass that grew around the doorstep. For a heartbeat I was sure he'd noticed, but he just snapped his lighter off and pocketed it.

'Thanks,' I said.

He gave a dismissive wave with his cigarette, then moved away a little, all while watching me.

Finally, the cops were done. They escorted me to the back of an unmarked station wagon and drove me down to the Moorabbin police complex for processing. They fingerprinted me before taking me into a tiny, cluttered room with a measuring decal on one wall. A new cop, one I didn't recognise, produced a camera and took a picture. 'Turn to your left,' he said. I turned to my right, and then, realising my mistake, started to spin, just as the camera went off, ruining the shot. The cop exploded: 'You trying to be a smartarse, fuckhead?'

'No, sir,' I said meekly. I turned to the left, then to the right, and he took two more shots. Years later I discovered that I wasn't obliged to be photographed and it was within my rights to sabotage the shot. The cop must have thought my twitching was a clever attempt to cheat the system, rather than terror-based spasticity.

Then the interview started. I was moved into a small room, maybe 5 metres square. It didn't look like an interrogation room from a movie, with cups of coffee and bribes of donuts and cigarettes from the good cop, and a two-way mirror with a feisty DA pacing behind it. There were no dark concrete walls blasted with light from a high-wattage interrogation lamp. Instead, with its worn carpet, cheap wood-particle table, plastic chairs and humming fluorescents, the room was exactly like those airless portable classrooms from high school.

Indeed, there was a general first-day-at-school feeling to the whole set-up: the two pissed-off authority figures staring at me over the table, and my sitting there awkwardly, ignorant of procedure, terrified of getting the etiquette wrong. I sat back in the chair and straightened up to make myself look taller, but then my feet didn't reach the ground. I swung them nervously back and forth under the chair.

I was terrified and when I'm nervous – on a date or about to get into a fight, for example – I have a bad habit of making jokes.

'So . . . do you come here often?' I tried.

Lacoste rolled his eyes. 'Let's get on with this, okay?' He placed an old-fashioned tape recorder on the table and pressed down the button.

Lacoste spoke, identifying the officers and me as being present in the room.

> Lacoste: Now, you've been found in possession of a trafficable quantity of a controlled substance . . .
>
> LP *(agreeable, happy to help)*: Yep!
>
> Lacoste: Along with scales, small plastic bags and other equipment consistent with dealing drugs . . .
>
> LP *(impatiently)*: Yes. Yep.
>
> Lacoste: Have you been dealing drugs?
>
> LP: For sure!

In my head I had already formulated a defence, which was, loosely: Yes, I am a drug dealer but only because I am a drug addict. I was using cannabis to self-medicate for the pain and trauma I felt over my brother's recent death. In truth, I didn't care for weed and hadn't touched it in months, but I thought that breaking the law to support my tragic habit would gain me better press than my real motivation, which was to buy nice jeans. So I told the cops all about my drug problem.

> Lacoste: So you regularly use cannabis?
>
> LP: Yes.

Lacoste: And how do you use cannabis?

LP: Oh, you know, I smoke it.

Lacoste: Mixed with tobacco?

LP *(snorting)*: Of course! I'm not a hippie.

Lacoste: And how long have you been using it for?

At this point I did some quick maths in my head.

LP: About . . . a year and a half.

Lacoste: And how often do you smoke it?

LP: Oh, you know, maybe three times a day.

Lacoste: So you've used cannabis three times a day for a year and a half?

LP: Yes, sir. That's me. Love my weed.

Lacoste: And how often would you say you sold cannabis?

LP: Oh, about . . .

Some part of me, the part that wasn't eighteen years old and thick as shit, was beginning to suspect I wasn't doing as well at this as I first thought.

Lacoste: Would you say you sold cannabis most days?

LP: Well . . .

Lacoste *(helpfully)*: To enable you to self-medicate?

LP: Yes, absolutely. Most days, probably, yes.

After a bit more of this, they produced the evidence one exhibit at a time, placing each item on the table in a plastic bag and asking me to identify what it was and what it was used for. Yes, that was my bag of cannabis; yes, it was intended for use and/or sale. Yes, those were my scales, with which I measured my cannabis for sale. Yes, this was my money, an amount of which was obtained through the sale of a controlled substance. Then the other bits of evidence were produced.

Lacoste put an A5 book with a lurid green cover on the table and asked me to read the title.

'*How to Grow Marijuana for Fun and Profit.*'

'Why do you have this book?' Lacoste asked.

This book, along with a well-thumbed copy of *On the Road* and some girlie mags, had been among my inheritance after we cleaned out Ardian's room. 'It was my brother's,' I said sadly.

'Have you ever grown marijuana?'

'No. Shit, I can't even grow tomatoes. Could never get them to sprout.'

And so on. Once the interview was over, I watched the exhibits go back into the box. *At least*, I thought, Bondage Fairies *isn't going to make it to court.*

They let me go, pending summons. My dad was waiting for me out the front of the complex. I climbed into the family station wagon and we drove home. He turned on the radio and cranked it up whenever a song he liked came on so he could sing along.

'Aren't you mad?' I asked him.

'A little,' he said kindly. 'But you've been through enough tonight.'

I smiled in the dark, looking out the window as we turned a corner away from the cop shop. My folks, for all their flaws, were there when I needed them.

'Plus,' he added cheerfully, 'they didn't find *my* stash.'

I got home and found my mobile ringing in the grass. I had a dozen missed calls from Sarah. I'd been lucky that she hadn't called while the police were still about. She was upset but not as upset as her mum. I can't remember what sort of outrageous lies I cooked up to get back in Mrs Lubow's good books, but she did let me back into her house, and even wrote me a reference for court later on. Bless her heart.

A few months later, I received my summons to the magistrates court. Because of my admission that I had used cannabis three times a day for a year and a half, and that I had sold it to cover the costs of this desperate need, I'd been charged with multiple counts of use of a controlled substance, and several counts of trafficking a controlled substance. I went to make myself a cup of tea and sat as the world rearranged itself into a wonderful, almost beautiful simplicity thanks to my dearth of options. Whatever happened next, I knew that, like the antagonists of *Bondage Fairies*, I was certainly, inescapably fucked.

13

The consensus among my friends and legal advisers was that I would be going to prison, where, with my schoolboy hips and dramatic cheekbones, I could expect to be repurposed to better suit the organisation, to appropriate the parlance of the HR department. To cheer me up, my friends hosted video nights where we would watch uplifting prison movies: *The Shawshank Redemption*, *Midnight Express*, *American History X*. I started to notice a recurring narrative trope.

I found myself marinating in permanent low-grade terror, the kind you build up to surgery. As the months passed, I almost became used to it. Since the law had caught up with me, I had finally given in to the realisation that with my 5-foot-nothing physique and floating vegetarianism, I wasn't a real criminal.

My parents tried to keep up my spirits, with stories about friends and heroes of theirs who hadn't minded prison and spent their time inside productively, learning new skills and making connections in the outside world. At the same time, they made me promise that I wasn't going to push drugs from under their roof any more. They needn't have bothered. Criminals are scurrilous gossips and the reality of my situation hit my networks faster than it did me. My phone, which had rung incessantly for the past year, fell silent the second I retrieved it from the garden after I'd returned from the cop shop.

My dealers, once they determined that I hadn't squealed on them and didn't need to be murdered, were sympathetic. Get a lawyer, they told me. Someone good. Get a Jew.

A friend of a friend knew a solicitor at a firm on Lonsdale Street. Their literature promised expertise in drug cases and enough experience to deliver 'the best possible outcome in the circumstances'. I called him, introduced myself and explained the situation. He listened, then asked a few questions.

'How much did they find you with?'

I told him.

'What about money?'

'About a grand. But only some of that was dirty —'

He cut me off. 'You should be very careful what you say on the phone, Liam. In fact, get off the phone. Come in and see me.'

He transferred me to a paralegal who booked a time for me to come in, then hung up. I sat in my bedroom holding the phone in my lap, listening to the purr of the dead line. It all seemed very, very real all of a sudden.

My meeting with the solicitor took fourteen minutes. He scanned through my summons and made an annoyed clicking noise against his teeth. As I sketched out the details, he sat tapping a legal pad with a pencil, occasionally making a note. He looked bored. When I was done he glanced at his watch.

'Listen,' he said, 'you're probably looking at some gaol time. It's a real possibility. It depends on what they end up pinning you with. You made a real mistake in talking. You should never talk to the police without a lawyer there. In fact, never talk to the police at all.'

He stood up and showed me to the door, talking as we walked. 'You're going to have to cease all illegal activity, which I'll assume you have already. On top of that, you'll stop taking all drugs and gather pathology to prove that. If you know any respectable people – lawyers, doctors, politicians, that kind of thing – get them to write you a reference.' We reached the elevator. 'Come here an hour before your hearing and we'll proceed to the magistrates court.' He looked me up and down and frowned at my jeans and raggedy jumper. 'And wear a suit. If you don't have a suit, a nice shirt and tie will do.' Then the doors closed and the elevator plummeted back to street level.

University started the next week. I'd done poorly at high school but still well enough to score a place studying social work at a university in the city. I had no idea what I was doing there beyond a vague idea that I wanted to 'help people'. In my mind this would involve guiding people through their drug and alcohol issues, presumably right after I'd sorted out my own. During the day I attended classes and listened to sociologists drone on about the causes of poverty and hardship, and at night I trawled through my address book trying to find someone who could serve as a character referee. A caseworker close to the family wrote me a reference, and a psychologist interviewed me and wrote the court a letter stating that in her professional opinion I was a bit crazy but prison would make me into a sociopath, and so she recommended a diversionary program.

I found it hard to make friends at university. I didn't fit in with either of the two broad schools of people studying social work. You had pretty young things from the country and fresh-faced private-school kids who all wanted to work in Ethiopia, and grizzled forty-somethings who had fucked up their lives and were looking to redeem themselves by warning others of their mistakes. I was your standard lefty humanities class warrior, with the chip on my shoulder furrowing ever deeper as I had to listen to sheltered young adults bang on about poverty and pathways to recidivism when I was probably going to prison at the end of semester.

On the advice of my solicitor, I was getting urine tests every few days to prove that I wasn't still smoking weed. This involved going to a pathology clinic where I had to give a 'supervised chain of custody sample', meaning I had to pee into a specimen jar while a pathology nurse watched in a carefully positioned mirror, like the ones they install in suburban train underpasses to prevent muggings. The supervision was necessary to assure the court that I was producing the sample myself and not tampering with it. The nurse had to keep a line of sight on me the entire time I was peeing so neither of us would break eye contact in that mirror, right up until the moment when I sealed the jar and passed it to them, still warm.

I usually got one of two nurses. The first was kind and matronly, with a trick where she seemed to look away, appearing professionally distant, even while standing by my side and using a pair of surgical forceps to hold my penis. The other nurse was about my age and the kind of cute, dark, bookish girl I tend to fancy, and who, predictably, I developed a crush on, which was its own kind of hell. Every time I handed over my Medicare card to her on the way out, smiling politely moments after she'd taken receipt of a jar of my warm, drug-addict's urine, I always felt like a pervert paying to have some horrible kink satisfied.

I became terribly nervous about the whole thing, and I often had crippling stage fright that prevented me from producing a sample – a problem that, as with most of life's little hiccups, I realised I could deal with by using drugs and alcohol.

When my first batch of results came back, I noticed I was only being tested for cannabis. They weren't checking for any other intoxicant and automatically marked those categories as 'negative'. The next day I had four beers before I went into the lab, where I produced a sample without a problem. Then, because I didn't want to go to university drunk, I had a few lines of blow to even myself out. The upshot of it all was that for the first semester of uni, while I was treading water and waiting for a judge to decide which underfunded government pen I would be spending the next few years in, my classmates had to suffer through my turning up merrily impaired, ranting about social strata and indentured servitude and inherited privilege, and only falling silent once the drugs had worn off. It was something of a revelation that I could spend the whole day drunk or high and still pull off a passable impersonation of a citizen. Sure, not a great citizen, but the booze and coke helped to ease the omnipresent terror, and I could relax enough to summon a facade of a personality when I needed to.

Half a year after my arrest, my day in court arrived. My family took the day off work and school to show solidarity, and made plans to meet me outside the magistrates court an hour before the contest mention. I woke up at dawn, showered, had a breakfast of toast and tea, wondering if this would be my last meal on the outside, and then put on the same charcoal-grey lounge suit I'd worn to my Year 12 formal. I arrived at my solicitor's office ten minutes before they opened and paced the pavement. I hadn't worn my school shoes since graduation and they bit into my heels as I stomped about. To distract myself I rocked back and forth, so that the creaky leather pinched my skin harder, and I relished the little burst of pain the way you do when you tongue a loose tooth in a dentist's waiting room.

When the doors opened I introduced myself to the receptionist and asked to speak to my solicitor.

She looked up at me. 'He's not in.'

'Oh. Is he already at the court?'

'He's in Hawaii.'

'Excuse me?'

'He's on leave.' She tapped at her keyboard. 'Until . . . next Monday.'

All the little threads of panic in my mind wove together into one magnificent, suffocating blanket. 'On leave?' I managed to choke out. 'He's supposed to be representing me in an hour.'

She sighed. 'What was your name again?'

'Liam. Liam Pieper.'

She turned to her computer again, typed something, and then her face fell.

'Shit,' she said, filling me with hope.

I spent the next ten minutes melting down in the mood-lit reception area until a bright-eyed young woman came up to me.

'Liam?' She was holding a folder with my name on it. 'I'm Lara. I'll take you to the magistrates.'

On the way we stopped for coffee, a complicated order of six different iterations of a flat white. She handed me a cardboard tray to carry and I tried to make small talk.

'How long have you been a lawyer?' I asked.

'Oh, I'm no lawyer!' She laughed. 'I mean, I'm doing my articles, but it's a while off yet.' At this point I made a pitiful little noise that made her whip around in concern. 'You'll be fine.' She smiled and squeezed my elbow encouragingly. 'I'm afraid your solicitor didn't tell us about your contest hearing before going on holiday, and we don't actually have anyone free to take your case.' She seemed slightly pissed off but still breezily professional. 'But that's okay. You don't need a solicitor, you need a barrister, and we can probably find you a barrister.'

Lara ushered me into the barristers chambers across the road from the court. I stood nervously in the lobby while she darted off to speak to a law clerk about finding me a representative.

One wall was decorated with portraits of distinguished barristers, past and present. I cast my eyes over them, noting the chronology from black-and-white photographs of stern old-world law-bringers in robes and wigs, through to modern guns, clean-cut and cold-eyed, all with the same expression. I looked away.

Lara came back, grinning. 'I found you someone!' She sounded excited and relieved at the same time. 'Just give him this.' She handed me the manila folder holding my brief.

My barrister was David, a good-looking, self-assured guy in his mid thirties, holding a coffee and rocking some stubble. He was hearteningly brisk in manner and soothingly Jewish in appearance. He shook my hand and took my case file. David opened the folder and scanned the contents, then let out a low whistle, the way a mechanic does when he pops the bonnet of your car to let you know he's about to rob you. He snapped the folder shut and tucked it under his arm. 'No problem. I'll meet you in there.'

Lara walked me to the magistrates court and shook my hand. 'Good luck,' she said brightly, which still sounded ominous. I went through the metal detectors and was patted down by security. I felt overdressed in my suit and my school shirt, which was starched so thoroughly it crackled when I fiddled with my tie. Many people were wearing nothing flashier than tracksuits and the monkeys on their backs.

A few bespoke-suited crims milled about with their entourages of friends, family and lawyers. They looked neither stressed nor relaxed, just bored and impatient to get on with burying people or stealing fortunes or whatever it was they did. Their comfort made me feel jealous. The only spare seat was next to a gentleman who'd rolled up his pant leg to pick at a scab. Instead, I just stood about until someone let me know my case was about to be heard. He pointed me towards a courtroom.

I shuffled in and caught the end of the preceding case, which happened to be a trafficking charge as well. A Vietnamese guy in his early twenties had sold a cap of heroin to an undercover officer. The cop detailed his case in clipped, officious policeman's speech, and the prosecutor reiterated it in polished, accusatory language. Then the dealer's lawyer stood up, a tired, harried legal aid guy, and laid out a simple guilty plea, mentioning a few extenuating circumstances, including that the kid was an addict and was only trying to support his habit and provide for his family.

My ears pricked up. This was the excuse I was planning to use. At the time I'd thought it highly original.

The judge was a red-faced, bearded man in his seventies. He looked like a retired rancher and erstwhile Klansman. He gave the kid three years.

Court broke for a fifteen-minute interlude. I went back outside to the waiting chamber and sat down heavily next to the chap with the troublesome leg. He'd picked off his scab entirely by this time and was dabbing at the wound with a napkin. I wondered if he would end up being my boyfriend once we were inside.

My parents and girlfriend entered the foyer. To show the judge what a normal, upstanding family we were, my folks had worn their finest office-party-in-1987 outfits, and Sarah looked dressed for synagogue in a modest ankle-length skirt and long-sleeved blouse. The combined effect was almost right, but subtly askew. I went to say hello and we stood about glumly. We all felt like we should say something meaningful.

'Thanks for . . . um . . . well . . . I'm sorry,' I tried. Sorry for what, exactly, I didn't know. Getting high? Selling pot? Getting caught? It just seemed like the appropriate thing to say. They, too, all tried their best.

Sarah: 'I'll wait for you – for a while.'

Dad: 'Many fine books have been written in prison.'

Mum: 'Hamish wants to borrow your leather jacket until you get out.'

We entered the Klansman's courtroom and took our seats in

the row set aside for the accused. The magistrate came in, trailing gin fumes and hellfire. I was, all things considered, feeling pretty good about the situation. Then, the main door opened and a line of teenagers in blazers trooped in. There is a truism at the magistrates court: whatever your crime, if there are schoolchildren in the courtroom, you will be staked out for the ants. The magistrate always goes harder on you when there are children around, as a cautionary example. I think I whimpered slightly. Then Lara tapped me on the shoulder.

'Follow me,' she whispered. 'I think I've got you another magistrate.' We followed her out and into another courtroom, where the clerk was calling my name. My barrister sat in front of us, playing with his phone. Lara appeared behind me and leaned over the bench to speak quietly in my ear. 'It's going to be okay. Trust me,' she said, and then disappeared. The prosecution read out the charges and the evidence in the same clipped, mechanical tones that the cop from the other courtroom had. There was my old buddy Lacoste from Moorabbin Regional. I just hadn't recognised him without his polo. He laid out his case, with some exhibits – *Bondage Fairies* thankfully withdrawn but the rest very much present.

Then the police prosecutor did his thing and I shit myself. Not literally, but very, very nearly. Actually, I don't know if I could have shit myself if I'd tried, all homeostatic functions deserting me in my panic, leaving me just an empty, quivering shell of a person. I could barely breathe.

Then my barrister did something amazing. He didn't try to plead my innocence, he didn't deliver an impassioned lecture on justice like some coked-up social-work student. He just stood up and spoke quietly and intently.

'This young man – this child – has freely admitted that he was a drug dealer, that he engaged in criminal behaviour. But he is not a criminal. No; he is a child. A child with a family and a loving girl-friend, here to support him.' He waved briefly to where my parents were sitting rigidly. 'The child of a family torn apart by tragedy: this boy's elder brother, his only role model, was snatched away from him by the very drugs that now threaten to ruin this boy's life.'

His voice softened and he looked up at the judge. 'All we ask, all I ask on his behalf, is that you consider what a criminal convic-tion would do to this boy, this budding social worker, if you decide to punish him for doing what he had to do to make life bearable.'

He sat down. I felt the room should have burst into applause. Perhaps it was on me to start a slow clap? But no, I was still para-lysed with fear. The police prosecutor made an exasperated coughing sound and my mum shot him a dirty look. The magistrate took a few minutes, shuffling papers, before addressing me.

'Would the defendant please rise?'

I rose. The magistrate was looking at me keenly. She had a soft, kindly face and sharp eyes. Those eyes were truly terrifying. Imagine eyes staring from the slit of a World War Two pillbox bunker, or the gloom of a childhood closet. I started trembling under her gaze. I wondered if she could see me shaking from up there.

'You've done some bad things, committed serious crimes, but I am not unaware of your extenuating circumstances.' She asked me how I planned to plead.

'Guilty, Your Worship.'

She nodded, and then said reflectively, almost conversationally, 'Tell me something, Liam. When you started smoking cannabis, did you know it was addictive?'

My eyes flicked over to my barrister. He gave the tiniest of nods and I looked down theatrically, before again meeting the magistrate's benevolent death stare.

'No, Your Worship. Not until it was too late.'

She banged her gavel and made her judgement.

I got lucky. Lara had steered me into the courtroom of Magistrate Jelena Popovic, who went on to become a crusader for harm minimisation in the field of drugs law. The same year, right-wing columnist Andrew Bolt lost a defamation case to her over a column in which he claimed she'd 'hugged two drug traffickers she let walk free' and she was awarded $246 500 in damages, plus costs. She never hugged me, but she did save my life. I floated out of the courtroom clutching a good behaviour bond. My ears were ringing and my blood was singing as all my adrenaline flushed out and turned sweet. I was free.

My barrister walked out.

'Shit!' he said, grinning. 'That went well.' Then he shook everyone's hand, like at a birth, congratulated me, and left.

I had a coffee with my family at a nearby café and then called my friends to tell them the news. That night I got high as a kite at a party a buddy threw at her apartment in town, where my friends lifted me up on their shoulders and gifted me a shirt that read, 'I got booked for trafficking and all I got was this stupid T-shirt.'

The next morning I stood on the roof of the apartment, smoking a cigarette and watching the sun rise over Melbourne. For the first time since Ardian had died I felt optimistic about the future. The dread of the court case had weighed so heavily on me that I hadn't noticed that my fatalism was waning. It turned out there could be outcomes other than tragedy and, for the first time in forever, I was looking forward to whatever was coming next. 'Okay,' I said out loud to the sunrise. 'That's enough.'

I was aware that I'd been given a second chance and I was determined not to waste it. I made a vow that I would never again touch drugs, an undertaking that lasted until I finished the cigarette and went downstairs.

ON THE ROCKS

14

Getting hauled through the court system didn't turn me into an upstanding citizen. Arresting someone, punishing them, incarcerating them: none of that teaches them the fundamental problem with committing crime. What it does teach them is not to get caught.

I had been rattled by my recent excursion, though, and decided that I was done with dealing drugs. That said, in the six months of terror preceding my trial I'd learned that when feeling anxious and having to do something taxing, such as, say, drive to uni, the best thing was to enjoy a bottle of vodka and a bump of coke. So I'd been dissuaded from pursuing a life of crime but I hadn't been scared straight – quite the opposite. My real takeaway message from the experience was that there is almost no situation in life that isn't easier to deal with after a couple of belts of something or other. I wasn't going to sell drugs any more, but I sure wasn't done taking them.

Another lesson was that maybe I wasn't the hard-boiled gangster I had assumed. This was confirmed for me when, a few months later, Sarah went to art school and took up with a guy in her class: a tall, skinny Nick Cave doppelganger who painted portraits of himself as Jesus on the cross. I walked in on them making out, started a fight and had my arse handed to me.

I walked away bleeding and downhearted. It hurt to catch Sarah with another guy, but I was more upset that I'd gone to defend my honour and been whipped. For years I had based my persona on being a kind of suburban ronin, whose deadly wit was matched only by his fists. Now I'd been dragged into the front yard of an Ormond townhouse and tenderised by a guy who painted with acrylics. *Acrylics.*

I wasn't cut out for a life of crime, and slowly, as my virtuoso-inflicted bruises started to fade, I began to realise this. My old associates and suppliers had distanced themselves from me, changing their numbers and switching up their codes, and my clients quickly moved on as other reprobates filled the gap I'd left.

Hamish, who'd been entertaining his friends and partners for years with an unlimited supply of weed and cash from my room, started casting further afield, and my parents went back to paying way too much on the ounce. All this seemed incidental to me at the time. Crime was the furthest thing from my mind. I was trying to get my life back together, which meant moving out of home and finding some kind of vocation.

Although I'd been a mediocre student my whole life, I did quite well in my first year at university. One of my tutors had mistaken my coked-out ramblings for passion, and I knew how to turn out an essay, which is all you need to be a humanities superstar. She took me aside to explain that she thought I could do some good as a social worker, so she had marked me higher than I deserved. I thanked her and then used the inflated grade to transfer out of social work and into an arts degree at a more prestigious university. I needed less direction and, besides, I figured my future social-work clients were better off without me.

I started moonlighting as a music critic and supplemented my income by working at a pizza shop. Once I had a few bucks, I set about to find myself, in all the usual ways. I hitchhiked up and down the east coast, wrote a terrible novel on an old laptop that was stolen from me by a burglar, thankfully before I had a chance to send the manuscript anywhere. Slowly, I healed what I was telling everyone was a broken heart but was really just a bruised ego.

That's when I met Katya. Katya was, in a word, Russian. She was diminutive, violent, sexy, vicious, brilliant and alcoholic. The first time I saw her she was standing on a table at a party, waving a bottle of Stolichnaya and screaming, 'WHO WANTS TO SEE SOME TITTY?' It was love at first sight.

She lived with her mum and step-dad, Vasily, a drunken, abusive retired Siberian soldier who ran a string of quasi-legal companies and collected *Scarface* memorabilia. Vasily was a properly bad man, a tightly wound ball of rage who could have tied me into a pretzel without breaking a sweat. When Katya was growing up, he would often beat his wife and step-daughter when he was drunk or just angry. After Katya and I had been seeing each other for a few months, Vasily revealed that he was having an affair with his wife's best friend. Then he ran up a couple of hundred thousand dollars in credit card debt, stole everything of value from their joint accounts and disappeared to Russia. I was looking to begin a new life, and so was Katya.

We got a flat together in a Russian ghetto in the south-eastern suburbs of Melbourne. We were both at university but Katya worked to support us while I wrote mediocre short stories, which brought in almost nothing. She got to know my family and I got to know hers, something I'd never really experienced with a girlfriend before, what with all the anxiety meds and police raids that had characterised my previous relationships.

I had no idea what I might do for a living. Between my general sloppiness and my legal troubles, I wasn't having to fend off potential employers with Sunny's trusty .22. My folks had, in their grief, more or less withdrawn from the world, only leaving the house to work or buy microwave dinners, so we weren't about to start a wholesome family business. In a way, actually, that's what had got me into this mess in the first place.

Surely, someone out there – an employer with deep pockets and the wisdom to appreciate my anti-authoritarian tantrums as a valuable corporate asset – would be willing to pay me to be me. It had to be that way. The alternative meant that blueprinting my life based on a Slim Shady album and *On the Road* was a mistake, and that was just unfeasible.

Following Ardian's death, friends and family became scarce in our lives. Sympathy is a finite resource, even for the most compassionate, and as the years passed and the world moved on, my parents remained moored in place by their grief as the rest of their lives broke apart and drifted off. If you've suffered an immense tragedy, a two-fisted, world-ending tragedy like losing a child, you never really get over it, in a way that most people can't understand. The cousins, uncles and family friends who supported you incrementally start to inch away from the exhaustive grief. They stop inviting you over because you can't stop crying. You turn down an invitation to a holiday abroad because where would you get hold of your not-quite-legal medication? You get into a fight over some bullshit because you're already strained to the point of breaking and stop speaking entirely. The loved ones who should be there to notice things have gone awry are absent, and you find yourself alone when trouble finds you.

So when looking for someone to emulate, Hamish had to improvise, and I was all he had, the poor bastard. On any objective scale I was a fuck-up – I drank far too much, I used drugs, I was a failed dealer – but that kind of thing looks good to a twelve-year-old. As he grew he started to walk with the same bouncy, effete caveman gait

I had going. When his voice broke it assumed the same mumbled cadence that mine has always had. I once talked to a shrink who told me I probably spoke that way because I'd learned English from people who were stoned most of the time.

Hamish talked a little faster, was a little quicker on his feet, a little more street smart when it came down to it, and maybe he was a little more considerate. Still, there were plenty of similarities that you couldn't help but notice if you put us side by side in, say, a police line-up.

He had, for instance, inherited my passion for intoxicants. Can't say I blame him. When he used to creep into my room to pinch weed and money, he found plenty of both, and I was always too wasted to notice. In later years I was angry when I realised just how much he had been stealing from me, and mortified when I realised he had also been reading the notebooks I wrote in that dark summer after I saw *8 Mile* and decided that I was a rapper.

By any metric, I was a shit big brother and a terrible role model; an exemplar of how you can succeed through laziness, selfishness, churlishness and vanity, if only you are ready to walk over enough people to do so. While this is absolutely true, and remains an important life lesson for many young heirs and heiresses of the world, it gives a middle-class hippie kid a poor grounding in life.

I used to throw parties every Friday night after school. My parents were from the harm-minimisation school of parenting. They figured, If the kids are going to do drugs and drink alcohol, they should do it at home, where we know they are safe. It's a good theory, but in practice it meant I had a polite beer and a spliff with them at the start of the night before sneaking off to my bedroom to rail crushed pills and try to convince Lilly to let my hand up her skirt. Around the time Hamish was starting high school, our house was more often than not filled with drunk and high teenagers dry-humping each other.

By the time Hamish was old enough to throw his own parties, my parents had rebuilt themselves enough to discipline him, but a precedent had been set and they were big on egalitarianism. As kids, whenever one of us had a birthday, the other siblings were given a 'jealousy present', some kind of tchotchke to stop us from fighting with each other. So if Hamish wanted to get drunk or high like I had, who were Mum and Dad to argue?

On his birthday, or even just when Mum and Dad were out of town for the weekend, I would buy Hamish booze or help him score drugs, then supervise in a half-arsed way that largely involved play-ing records and flirting with his friends. If there was trouble I would sort it out, and I usually invited a couple of my more thuggish friends around in case things got nasty.

It only got really rough once and that was my fault entirely. I was supervising one of Hamish's parties while my parents were away at some crystal-healing retreat, when a hoard of FUBU-clad teens gate-crashed. In a panic I called the Ryans to tell them I had a problem. Ten minutes later, two Commodores came screeching into our street and a dozen martial artists got out and started beating the shit out of the teenagers. It was kind of beautiful to watch, if terrible, like a David Attenborough documentary in which seagulls pick off baby turtles as they amble towards the ocean. A handful of wiry fighters grabbed the wiggers by the scruffs of their necks and marched them out of the party. There wasn't much fightback, except for two lads who pulled out trolley poles. They dropped them, though, when one of the Ryans unsheathed his katana. In retrospect, I'd overreacted.

'Look, Liam,' one of the Ryans explained to me diplomatically. 'We're happy to come down and help you when you're in trouble, but you're only really supposed to call us in emergencies.'

My fraternal instincts were patchy at best. Everything I did to make life better for my little brother just laid the groundwork for something much worse further down the line.

By 2006 I had, if not sobered up, then got a handle on my drinking and drug intake, wrangled a BA out of university, found work in kitchens, fallen in love, moved in with my girlfriend, and saved up enough cash to go overseas for the first time. Katya and I pooled our money, bought round-the-world tickets and packed up our apartment, ready to spend a year circumnavigating the globe. There was a gap of a couple of weeks between when we ended our lease and our jetting off. By coincidence, my folks were away on holiday, so we moved into the family home – just me, Katya and Hamish.

It wasn't a smooth fortnight. Hamish's friends were always around the house, smoking cones and railing lines, and while many of them were charming young men and women with interesting theories on *The Matrix*, the rest were fucking cunts. I kicked out one pituitary case for stealing the change from Katya's wallet after she'd left it on the coffee table, and I was forever talking some poor young lady who'd taken too much acid down from the roof – figuratively, most of the time.

The day before we were due to fly out, our friends threw us a going-away party in town. I'd recently done a review for a magazine that couldn't pay me but offered to settle the account with beer. I found myself in possession of a station wagon full of slabs, too much to drink in one night, so I took as much as I could carry in a taxi to the party and gave the rest to Hamish as a peace offering for putting up with me for the past few weeks.

Our flight was at 10 a.m., and our party went all night. As gloom lifted over the city skyline that morning, Katya and I kissed our friends goodbye, climbed in a taxi and headed for the suburbs to pick up our luggage before flying to Argentina. As the cab pulled up near our house, I saw the all-too-familiar wash of blue and red lights over our street. A half-dozen or so emergency vehicles were parked out the front of the family home.

'Fuck,' Katya said. 'What has that *pisda* done now?'

A police sergeant came towards me as I was climbing out of the cab.

'Are you Liam Pieper?'

'What seems to be the problem, officer?' I felt the catechism spill out of my mouth – something I've never been able to refrain from saying to cops. It's one of those verbal tics, like when a waiter tells me to enjoy my sandwich and I cheerfully scream at him, 'YOU TOO!'

'The problem is that your little brother and his friends have stolen your car.'

Do you know the feeling of drawing a losing hand on a huge bet in poker, and your heart fills with fury and despair, all while you try to smile winningly? That.

'I don't think so, officer. They wouldn't do a thing like that.' The cop grinned, then pointed up the street. I craned my head to peer around the corner block where he was pointing, to see my car twisted around the remains of a brick fence three doors up. I could see it quite clearly in the flashing lights, the front wheels well over the ruins of the low wall, with the chassis balancing precariously on a mess of crumbled brick and the twisted guts of my station wagon. I stared at it agape for a minute while the situation clawed its way into my foggy brain. The cop was waiting on me, smug but cross and tired. Next to me, I felt Katya start to vibrate with Slavic fury.

'That little shit!' she hissed. 'Where is he?'

'That's a good question,' the cop said. 'He's done a runner.'

My mind kicked into gear, the way my poor car never would again. 'Officer, I don't believe my little brother would do this. What evidence do you have?' Somewhere along the line I'd developed the habit of speaking in overly formal, almost Edwardian English when talking to police. The cop sighed and started his inventory, counting off on his fingers as he went.

'We have a positive ID from a neighbour who saw the vehicle leave the garage and drive through the fence. The same neighbour, in fact most of the neighbourhood, has identified your brother as running from the vehicle. Your keys are still in the ignition, and your brother has left his wallet in the vehicle. A few minutes after the incident, he called 000 to report the car as having been stolen while he was asleep. We're pretty sure he's inside the house, but nobody is answering the door.'

It did seem persuasive when you put all the facts in a line like that, but I said, 'I'm not convinced, but if this has happened like you say, what are you going to charge him with?'

'That depends on him. If he turns himself in, we'll charge him with driving without a licence and probably driving under the influence. Otherwise, we'll catch him and charge him with a whole lot more, starting with insurance fraud.' The cop turned to leave. It was late in his shift and he obviously wanted to go home. I could see in his eyes that mentally he was already tucked up on the couch in his trackies, catching up on TV. 'If you see him, I'd do my best to get him to turn himself in. Otherwise you'll all be hurting.'

My parents had a thing for native plants. The house was ringed by a thicket of native ferns and low-lying shrubbery that was popular with giant spiders. At night all throughout my childhood I could hear the spiny branches of the ferns scraping against the windows whenever the breeze picked up. Functionally, the thicket made it difficult to get near the windows of the house, so unless someone actually opened the door, it was next to impossible to determine whether anyone was home. This had its benefits, like when Jehovah's Witnesses or door-to-door salesmen – or the police, for that matter – dropped around.

I unlocked the back door and stepped into the lounge room. It was dark and the air was thick with cigarette and bong smoke. On each of the two couches was a teenager wrapped up in a sleeping bag. It felt like that moment at a slumber party when somebody's angry dad walks in and you all lie dead silent and pretend to be asleep.

I rolled one of the kids over. It was Tim, one of Hamish's friends who I'd seen chasing shots with beers earlier in the night. He made a show of waking up groggily.

'Liam?' He blinked and smacked his lips like a cartoon character. 'Hey! What's happening? Did something happen?' He would have been more convincing if he didn't have the big teddy-bear eyes and grinding jaw of someone who'd been up on drugs for a very long time.

Katya leaned over and smacked him across the face. 'Don't fuck around, you little cunt!' she snarled. 'Where is Hamish?'

All the air went out of the kid. 'I don't know,' he said miserably. 'He took off running when the cops arrived. We didn't mean to crash your car. We just wanted to get some cigarettes.'

'Where did he go?'

'I don't know. He just ran out the back door.' The poor guy was close to tears. 'He hit his head when we stacked the car. He was bleeding.'

Katya and I were due at the airport in less than an hour, each of us with a non-refundable $8000 round-the-world ticket. We called the airline to ask if we could defer the flight and they flat-out told us no. They explained that the flight could not be pushed back, that it was company policy for the ticket to be forfeited if an international flight was missed. Given that we couldn't afford another ticket, we had to get on that flight, or we didn't leave at all. My fantasies about strolling through the cobblestoned streets of Buenos Aires, stopping to shoot the breeze with tango dancers in Spanish, or make love to tango dancers, also in Spanish, evaporated. I thought of the pastries I wouldn't buy from cute corner shops and the tasteful but inexpensive antique Spanish silver I wouldn't buy from street vendors to take home for all my loved ones to admire.

Dazed, I let go of Tim's neck, and he rolled himself back into a ball and pretended to be asleep again. I wandered to the front of the house, checking the bedrooms to see if Hamish was in any of them. I opened the front door and slumped on the porch to smoke a cigarette as gravity set in.

I flashed back to Ardian laid out cold on the slab, his blood black against blue skin, and suddenly it was Hamish. In the minute I spent fumbling with my cigarettes, I saw my little brother die a dozen times. He succumbed to a head injury and bled out in some flophouse. He realised too late that he needed help, trying to stand on shattered legs, bones protruding through ruptured skin. The pigs grabbed him and he died after being shivved in a holding cell. Or he ran from the cops again and they opened fire. My hands were shaking as I lit the cigarette.

Then Hamish jumped out from behind a fern.

The cigarette fell out of my mouth and lay for a second on my jacket, burning a hole into it, before I recovered enough to let out a strangled cry of relief. Then I pulled Hamish into the house and started choking him.

It had happened like this. Hamish and his friends had drunk a slab, and then another, then several more. At a certain point they'd run out of cigarettes. A few of them, Hamish included, were eighteen, but none had a driver's licence or any other kind of ID, so they couldn't get cigarettes. Then one of them had an idea. If they drove to a 7-Eleven and the guy behind the counter could clearly see that they were 'driving' a 'car' like 'adults', then that would be incontestable proof that they were eighteen.

The keys to my station wagon were in my room. I'd figured I wouldn't need them on my trip, so I'd stowed them away and cancelled the insurance before mothballing the car in the garage. The station wagon also had a sticky clutch, which I'd put off repairing until I returned in a year's time. When they stole the car none of them had never driven before, the clutch jumped and it went straight out of the carport, across the road and through the neighbour's fence.

Hamish had cracked his forehead on the dashboard but remained conscious. He and Tim sat dazed, looking at each other, and then leaped out of the car and back into the house. They spent a couple of much panicked minutes making a plan and then acting on it.

They would call the police to report that the car had been stolen while all the young men in the house were asleep. To add gravitas to the story, Hamish would affect a sleepy *What the hell is going on here?* demeanour. Ever the method actor, he got into his pyjamas and jumped into bed before Tim dialled 000.

'Hi . . . um . . . This is Tim. I'm a friend of Hamish Pieper's. He's Liam Pieper's little brother. Um . . . I think someone just stole Liam's car. I'm just waking Hamish up.'

At this point, Hamish picked up the receiver and said sleepily into the phone, 'Hello? This is Hamish. What's going on? Did someone steal Liam's car?'

Hamish was transferred to the local police station, where they said words to the effect of 'We know you stole the car, Hamish. We're outside.' The cops then banged on the front door.

Hamish opened it, doing his best to smile beatifically.

'We know you did it.'

'That's crazy! I didn't do anything.'

'We have a witness who saw you crash the car then come inside this house.'

'Oh.'

'Do you have a photo we can show the witness?'

'Um . . .'

'Or we can pull up your file. We know you have priors.'

'Wait here. I'll get the photo.'

Hamish closed the door, and then took off sprinting out the back. He doubled back midway around the block, sneaked under the house and hid in the fern garden while the cops did a perfunctory search of the area but kept away from the mess of plants and huntsman spiders that Hamish was hiding in. He was watching while I spoke to the cops, and once they'd left he jumped out and explained it all to me.

Now that I'd confirmed Hamish was still alive, I had to decide quickly how to kill him. I also had less than half an hour to be at the airport, if I was going to fly. Hamish was on the run from the cops, my folks weren't back to look after him for another two weeks, and, although his head wound wasn't severe, he was in serious danger of being eviscerated by Katya. She stalked back and forth, small and vicious, rippling with muscle, like a badger about to skin a vole.

'What are you going to do?' I asked him.

'I don't know,' he mumbled.

I lost my temper. 'Well, figure it out in a hurry! You little shit! Do you even know what you've done?' I wanted to hit him.

'Yes.'

'Are you going to turn yourselves in?'

He balled a fist and hit himself in the head twice. Then he lifted his chin to look at me. 'I'm going to kill myself.'

I spoke softly, my voice dropping in the way it only does when I'm very, very angry. 'You aren't going to do that. Because that's self-ish and childish and now you have to be a fucking man and own this.' I thought for a minute. 'You are going to go and stay at Tim's house until Mum and Dad get home. Then you are going to tell them what you've done and together you guys are going to hire a lawyer and sort this out.' I drew a deep breath and let it out. Hamish was staring miserably at the ground. I felt cool now, hard and empty as a Sherrin. 'I'm going to Argentina.' I shook Hamish's hand, stiff and formal and awkward – we'd never shaken hands before. 'Fix this,' I told him, and on my way out the door I pulled Tim aside and whispered in his ear. 'Watch him. If he hurts himself, I'll kill you.'

And I was gone.

On the fourteen-hour flight to Argentina, I felt like the biggest piece of shit in the world. I'd abandoned my little brother in his hour of need, and as I hurtled to the other side of the world I had no idea if he was in police custody or not. I'd suspected for some years that I was a selfish person, and now, when the crunch had come, I'd turned my back on my family right when they needed me the most.

After we landed the first thing I did was call home. It rang out and kept ringing out for two weeks while I tore out my hair. Finally, Hamish picked up the phone.

'Oh, yeah, I'm fine,' he said cheerfully. 'The cops have been around a few times but I just didn't answer the door. They can't touch me.'

And so they couldn't. They interviewed him a few days after the incident, and Hamish explained that he'd put the keys in the ignition of the car in order to use the headlights to light the party, then forgotten to retrieve them. A passer-by must have seen the car and opportunistically stolen it, only to crash into the fence. He finished the story and smiled at the officer taking notes.

'Well, it appears to us that you are the perpetrator. You have to admit, Hamish, that these are very suspicious circumstances.'

'I didn't do it.'

'I'd bet my left nut that you did.'

'Well, then you'd be out of a nut. I suggest you check with your good lady-wife before you go putting any bets down.' The cops let him go, reluctantly.

They tried again once Mum and Dad had returned home, laying out the facts, but my parents weren't hearing any of it. They rounded on the cops and delivered a lecture on Hamish's innocence. 'He would never drive a car without us there! He's simply terrified of driving. What you're alleging is impossible.'

Shortly afterwards Dad wrote me a long, angry email letting me know that my car had been stolen because I'd left the keys in the ignition, how stupid that was, and how disappointed he was in me, and what a bad example I was setting for Hamish. I wrote back to say I would try to be a better role model in the future, and to say hi to Hamish for me, and that I was looking forward to catching up with him for a chat when I got home. Then I went out for a walk through the cobblestoned streets of Buenos Aires, looking for somewhere to practise my Spanish and for someone who might sell me a tasteful but inexpensive pistol to bring home.

15

They say that travel is the surest way to find out what you are made of. As it turns out, I'm fashioned from some kind of adamantine alloy of cocaine and Bacardi. What I discovered about myself in South America is that, given unlimited quantities of these substances, I will keep taking them forever.

In Peru, specifically, I crossed over from what might be considered a casual to a binge drug user. Whenever I touched drugs or alcohol, the first part of my brain to turn off was the part that told me to stop taking drugs. That meant I kept drinking and smoking and snorting until I passed out, which, really, meant that we were out of drugs, and there was no way to get more, and there was no one around to play with. If I was responsible, I would say that addiction made me keep doing drugs long after they were no longer fun, but of course that's bullshit. They're always fun. That's the point.

It was about taking uppers and downers to find that perfect alchemical teetering point where I was neither too high nor too low. I might do a line of cocaine to sober up, or drink to soothe the nagging edge of an amphetamine downturn. Think of seasoning a stew right at the end of the cooking process, the tricky part where you have to try to bring out the flavours without oversalting it. It's safe to say that by the time I creaked back into Melbourne at the end of the year, I'd well and truly broken my off switch.

Just as every generation thinks it discovered sex, my friends and I thought we'd invented the concept of days-long partying, and we approached it with the full enthusiasm of youth. My moral system was rewritten, one component at a time, and that little voice inside my head that told me, Maybe don't snort that off a toilet seat, and, Let's reconsider stealing from the till of this unsatisfying retail job to buy rock, and, Perhaps let's not sleep with our partner's friends, became less and less assertive.

In June 2006 there was a random Bolivian hotel room that I didn't leave for days because I was too high to remember where I was staying. When security finally kicked me out for throwing a pot plant at some guy because he refused to stop playing Oasis's 'Wonderwall' on guitar, I realised that I'd been partying in my hotel all along, a few doors up from my own room.

And then there was the New Year's Day party back in Melbourne where we forcibly removed our drug dealer for flipping out and choking a girl, and then found he'd left behind a $5000 bag of amphetamine, which we spent the next week smoking in a fit of righteous pique. 'Give me that crack pipe! Let's teach that arsehole a lesson!'

Six months after that, frazzled and strung out on cocaine, I kissed another woman and embarked on a great, rollicking adventure in loneliness and deprivation in which I abandoned Katya, pawned the life we'd built together and moved out of the home we shared only to realise I had nowhere to go.

For a while I crashed on friends' couches, then I spent a month on a mattress at my parents' house before my brother's ghost found his way into my dreams and I stopped sleeping.

Getting a place of my own proved tricky. I didn't have the paper trail a good citizen is supposed to. I had no history of gainful employment and my name had never been on a lease; Katya had always been the grown-up in our relationship. It's not as though I had enough money to pay rent and bond anyway.

I didn't have much luck finding a room in a share house either. I couldn't sleep if I'd had less than half a litre of vodka, and it was hard to wake up without a little eye-opener. I'd turn up to the interviews drunk or high or hungover, and if I didn't reek of booze, the housemates could smell the desperation on me. It was obvious at a glance that I was not quite right.

I went to one interview in Flemington that seemed to be going well. It was a nice, well-appointed house with three flatmates, a reasonable-sized bedroom and a big kitchen. It even had a pool. We were sitting by the pool, discussing internet options, when the interviewer looked down and yelped, 'Holy shit! What's wrong with your hand?'

I looked in surprise at my right hand. I'd completely forgotten that I'd mangled it in a drunken fracas the night before. I'd picked out the glass and bandaged it up prior to driving to the interview but now blood was oozing through the gauze.

'Oh.' I thought fast. 'That was a sporting accident.'

'Sporting?'

'Soccer. But . . . you know . . .' I stumbled. 'The kind where you use your hands.'

I didn't get that room, or any other, and I went back to crashing at my folks' house.

Then one day, while I was having tea with my grandmother, she mentioned that an aunt, someone connected to me by one tendril of the nebulous web of marriage and divorce and Catholic roulette that made up the extended family, had an investment property she wasn't doing anything with. I called her to ask if she would be interested in renting out the house. There was a long pause at the other end. 'Sure,' she said eventually, sounding surprised. 'Why not?'

The house had seen better days: specifically, the day it was built. It had been in precipitous decline ever since. When it had been erected, at the end of the seventies, it was a magnificent family home nestled among the doctors' offices and colonial bluestones of Malvern.

It had been featured as the 1979 House of the Year in *Better Homes and Gardens* magazine, as a paragon of architecture and good taste, but hadn't seen a maintaining hand since. It still had its original fittings – stained-glass windows, chandeliers, two grand fireplaces, including a wood stove embedded in a load-bearing pillar in the middle of the lounge room – but they had all gone to seed. The house had been abandoned some time in the 2000s, and then slumped into undignified middle age.

Wall-to-wall shag-pile carpeting had long since matted into one springy dreadlock. The foundations had given way and the floor slanted dramatically from south to north. The house had two bathrooms, one of which had been annexed by a family of possums. Generations of ivy had covered the house in a carapace of petrified vines, penetrated the long-dead central-heating ducts and punched in all the windows on the top floor. The vines actually added some structural integrity to the place. It was held together by living plants and asbestos.

I spotted some of the carcinogenic plasterboard while being given the grand tour.

'Say,' I said, pointing to a wall. 'Is that asbestos?'

My aunt, who was walking through the house, enthusing about the vintage style of the place, paused.

'Yes,' she said. 'But that's blue asbestos. The good kind. What you want to watch out for is green asbestos.'

There was plenty of both colours and more in the backyard, which had once been a carefully landscaped garden and was now a *Mad Max*–esque wasteland of abandoned building materials and burned-out fridges. Great piles of red, blue and green cladding, the full rainbow of asbestos, were loosely covered in corrugated iron. If I scraped away the detritus underfoot, I could see rough-hewn bluestone cobbles etched with the initials of the convicts who had laid them. The whole place reeked of decay, despair and abandoned dreams.

'It's perfect,' I said.

I called around and put together a team of people who were willing to rent rooms in what was essentially a squat for a couple of bucks a day. Jules and his cousin Darce each took a room, as did Lilly. We all had our problems: Darce loved his booze a little too well; Jules had a broken heart; Lilly needed a career change. Mine were a happy mix of all of these.

For a while things had a dingy cheeriness. Jules bought a piano and wheeled it into the lounge room. Someone's cousin donated some furniture and at night Darce and Jules would stay up late drinking and writing songs, breaking up old chairs we found in the backyard for firewood. One night we got drunk and Darcy painted a 3-metre-high portrait of Miles Davis on the wall. *That's a fucking great idea!* I thought, and we painted every wall in the house with a portrait of a different jazz musician.

It was a little bit Kerouac and a little bit Dickens. If I tried hard enough I could pretend it was all an adventure rather than a desperate last-ditch attempt to rebuild my life. The boys called the place 'the Dog Pound', which eventually just became the Pound. We didn't have the energy to keep prefacing 'pound' with 'dog'; we needed every calorie we could get to maintain body heat.

It was a dark time. Winter settled over the Pound. The front door had been ripped off its hinges so the wind whipped through the house. If I went to sleep with a glass of water by the bed, it would be iced over in the morning. The fraying, frostbitten bohemia kindled a sense of nostalgia for my childhood at Labassa, but nostalgia wouldn't keep me warm.

During the day I sat by the fire, and at night I slept underneath a doona and a pile of coats on top of a futon. I was luxuriating in my wretchedness. I wanted anyone who happened to walk by to know that I was a broken man. Looking back, I guess it was an instinctive effort to get someone to notice and take care of me. I remember bringing a woman I'd been seeing back to my house. She looked around in amazement before telling me, 'I can't believe you would bring a girl here! What's wrong with you?'

As it happens, there is a certain kind who finds a truly broken person irresistible. For a couple of years my whole game was to corner women, dump the bleeding stump of my heart on the table and make keening noises until they tried to fix it. Each party I went to would end in a contest of one-upmanship with someone sporting prison tatts about who'd had the shittier life, and eventually we would just sleep together. A lot of these women were very sweet: retired junkies, gaolbirds, survivors of broken homes. If someone tells you they 'had a rough childhood', what they really mean is that they are 'good in bed'.

Around that time a shrink I sometimes scored weed for convinced me that my problems with substances were the result of trauma-related intimacy issues. 'Think how much time and energy you put into these quick-fix solutions: alcohol, cocaine. What is it that you think you're searching for? Think how different your life would be if instead of chasing these brief highs, you put your energy into building relationships.'

She's right! I thought. *I can fuck my way right out of this mess!*

There's a comfort in strange skin, in feeding a hunger that is mindless and endless, so I started sleeping around in earnest. What followed was a confusion of relationships that stacked and overlapped and failed. I started reaching out to people the way I did to bottles and powders. At the right time, as the night threatens to break into horrible dawn, a kiss is as good as a crack pipe.

Of course, that isn't a particularly wholesome way to live. Before long the whole concept of sex had divorced itself from intimacy and soured into something more utilitarian. Whenever I met a potential new partner, I must have looked like a human being receptive enough to the idea of a proper relationship, but in terms of emotional intelligence I was a neutered dog begging under the table for scraps.

My drug abuse and my womanising exacerbated each other. When I had coke I was – in my own eyes at least – charming and sparkling, the life of the party, and when I didn't I was morose and withdrawn. Often I would meet someone nice at a bar and invite them home, only to degenerate from an excitable, eager-to-please lad into a twitchy, sullen Gollum in the space of a taxi ride.

Coke made me feel alive, heightened every sense, leaving my skin tingling with bacchanalian pleasure, at least for the first few lines. One of the problems with coke is that it floods you with dopamine, taking away all your fear, doubt and any concept of limitations. If you look at brain scans of people staring into the eyes of their true loves, or mothers holding their newborns, they bear a startling similarity to those of people under the influence of cocaine. That's why coke is the drug of choice for movie stars, footy players, politicians, anyone with skewed morality and an underdeveloped sense of self. Coke is like a hug for big babies.

The blast of dopamine given by even the most stepped-on, adulterated powder makes you feel superhuman long after you've been physically reduced to a grey-skinned, mumbling, jaw-grinding troll. The disconnection between the inside and the outside of a coke binge is remarkable. Once you've passed a certain threshold, for example, you can't think of anything much except sex, even as your body goes into extremis. By the end of a long day on the powder, you have as much chance of banishing sexual thoughts as you do achieving an erection. I can't tell you how many evenings I spent crouched over some poor lady, full of sound and fury, whispering sweet, sexy nothings, wanking furiously, completely impotent.

It wouldn't have taken a genius to work out I wasn't ready for a relationship. A simple blood test could have said as much. I'd always been a little frayed at the edges, but now I was in the throes of a pounding drug psychosis and unravelling fast, all while using the affections of women who deserved better as novelty Band-Aids, desperately plastered over the gaping deficit in my humanity. Take a man whose moral fibre is threadbare, find a seam and pull, and you've got a pretty good look at me back in those days.

When someone I was seeing asked me to be their boyfriend I would always say yes, but I would never stop sleeping with other people. Instead I would lie. At one point I was seeing six different women at once. To my coke-addled mind it seemed easier to juggle them than to break up with any of them. To make things more manageable, I'd give them all the same pet name – 'Honey', or something like that – then bulk message them from my Nokia. Typically, I would wake up at one woman's house, have brunch at another's, and then head off for an afternoon nap at a third's, and so on. I was unscrupulous, not just in how I treated these women but also in the way I fixated on how they could help me.

At the time I couldn't see that what I was doing was wrong. Or, rather, I knew I was making mistakes, that my actions were inexcusable – I just didn't care. You have to be careful when you live a lie that it doesn't become too easy. Lying is like drinking. Once you have the hang of a double life, it's really not that much harder to make it a triple, or a quintuple.

When I was high it didn't occur to me that promiscuity could have a downside. If I'd been just a little honest, just a little decent in my dealings with people, then it might have been different. I still had a lot of fun, though. Whenever I see a movie that tries to portray the grittiness of addiction with a clumsy, raw sex scene, I can't help but feel they're missing the point. Those clumsy, raw sex scenes were the greatest. Sex and drugs go together like rock and roll and drugs. Or the night sky and drugs. Or screensavers. Or pretty much anything with drugs. Anyone who has served as a coke tray for two women, one blonde and kind-hearted, the other dark and competitive, has no cause to complain about the hand life has dealt them.

The real tragedy of addiction is what you steal from other people. I don't mean money, or property, or drugs – although I stole plenty of each to keep up my habit – it's the time. An addiction will use up your time, years of your life that you will never get back. And it steals time from those who care for you. I know plenty of people who could enjoy a cheeky evening on the old crack pipe with next to no consequences, and that's fine. I could never manage that. For years I thought that I could carry my madness around and keep it a secret, unaware that it was plain to see, that the people I thought were buying my act when I lied and cheated weren't idiots – they just cared for me. I abused their trust, disavowed their love and, worst of all, stole their time, wasted their days. Whether it was a couple of months or a couple of years, each of those people deserved better.

In the end, it wasn't creeping maturity, or bitter consequence, nor a wrathful God or woman that brought my sleeping around to an end, but that old chestnut, anxiety. Idly browsing the internet before bed,

I read a story about a sex addict who'd been infected with HIV via a blow job from a rent boy with bleeding gums. At the end of the article, I said to myself, *Isn't that interesting. I didn't know you could catch HIV while* getting *head*, then I put on my pyjamas, fixed myself a cup of chamomile tea, turned in and woke up screaming.

I'd had pretty good luck with STIs in the past. Despite my promiscuity, I'd more or less escaped incurable venereal complaints. Now, though, convinced I had contracted HIV in at least a dozen places, I went to the doctor to have myself checked. I described exactly what had happened and he told me he would run some blood tests, but that it was almost inconceivable I would have HIV. It was more likely I was having a panic attack.

'Liam, is there any kind of traumatic past event that you may not have dealt with fully yet?'

'No. Not that I can think of.'

'Would you be open to the idea of seeing a psychologist?'

'. . .'

'Or I could write you a prescription for something that would —'

'Yes, please. I'll take the pills.'

He sent me home with a clean bill of health and a bottle of Valium.

Then about a month later I noticed something as I was drying myself off after a shower. Despite my half-arsed spiritualist upbringing, I still have a classically Catholic relationship with my body, which means that, except for the occasions when I'm masturbating and crying shamefully, I like to ignore it. When bathing, I'll give myself a once-over to check that I'm not sporting any major wounds, then quickly dress and leave the Cartesian duopoly to the experts. This time, however, I spotted that something was wrong with my penis.

On its surface were tiny red sores: angry little craters spaced out on the lunar whiteness of my manhood. With my foreskin pulled back in my chilly bathroom, my little Liam looked for all the world like the *Super Mario* mushroom. I freaked out and reached my GP's surgery in record time, my hair still wet from the shower.

The GP, a true professional and one of the finest physicians I've found in the kind of 'hot chocolate in the vending machine and knife wounds in the waiting room' bulk-billing clinics I frequented, saw the state I was in and ushered me through without hesitation. He donned gloves and took the offending article between thumb and forefinger and played with it briefly, rolling it between his digits as though it were a lump of blue-vein cheese from a fromagerie he didn't quite trust. 'Yes,' he sighed at last. 'You have molluscum contagiosum. It's a localised viral infection.'

'What?' I squealed. At this point I would like to state that I normally take bad news with rugged stoicism, but I'd never had an STI before. Besides, the doctor was rubbing my testicles. 'What does that mean? Did I catch it from sex?'

'No, no,' he laughed, which reassured me, although customarily I'm down on people laughing while touching my junk. 'This rarely presents as an infection of the genitals. Normally it affects other areas. In fact, I've never seen a man's genitals infected. It is highly infectious and spread by touch, but usually this illness affects children between ages one and ten, who get it on their hands. If you'd like me to talk to your partner —' I cut him off with a polite no, and he went on to explain that the infection was easy to treat, by burning each of the 36-odd lesions with dry ice, and then scraping the blisters off with a blade.

He worked quickly, but it was still a long, long process. At the slightest touch of scalpel or icy cotton swab, my penis contracted, shrivelling into a pensive acorn. To get between the wrinkles, the doctor had to stimulate the glans until the shaft became turgid – the kind of rubbery half-mast erection common to the nervous and the drunk, a swan's neck rising from the lake. I lay back while the doctor performed his medical-grade hand job, stopping every once in a while to hack away at me with ice and steel. To pass the time we made small talk.

'So . . . do you read?'

'Not really . . . Do you like footy?'

'No. I don't mind soccer though.'

'Don't watch soccer. Bunch of wankers if you ask me,' said the doctor, jerking me off. He took a break to refresh his dry ice, which gave me the chance to thaw. I started to feel bad for myself, and for the first time I regretted having slept around so much. I'd always been quietly (read: loudly) proud of my sexual prowess. Now, lying shrivelled in the doctor's palm, my dick looked like an abandoned yum cha dish.

Then, at long last, it was done. The doctor walked me out and I shook his hand gingerly at the door. He wished me well and added, 'You might want to keep it in your pants for a while. I mean, that's not my professional opinion. It's just good advice.'

Good advice, like good intentions, meant precisely fuck-all to me at the time. What I needed was to stop acting on the crashing, disastrous orders my brain had been dishing out for the past decade, but that's not what I wanted. I didn't want to be sober, I wanted to be anything but, and I had surrounded myself with people who would help me to do that. At the age of twenty-five, I was spending my time with anyone who could get me high. I was long past caring about who they were or what kind of damage we were doing to one another. Apart from those who had been foolish enough to move in with me, my real friends were all gone by now, tired of my shit. The times we'd shared and the memories we'd built were left on the cutting-room floor as I edited my life into a version that let me get on with wasting it.

16

I first met the Artist on the balcony of my drug dealer's apartment. It was the middle of a particularly brutal Melbourne winter. She'd just moved to the city and was huddled inside her coat, shivering. We were seventeen storeys up and our breaths frosted in the air as we spoke, before being whipped away by the bitter winds that stole across the skyline, and we decided we should be friends.

A few months down the line, she called me. It was about 10 p.m. and I was in bed reading when the phone went.

'Liam! Thank God you're awake! We're having a party. Can you come over?'

'Sure.'

'Can you bring a friend?'

'Our mutual friend?' This was code, clearly. 'Friend' was shorthand for 'bag of drugs' in our impenetrable argot. Take that, Navajo code talkers.

'Yes, please.' I heard her take the phone away from her ear and parts of a muffled conversation at the other end. 'Actually, better make that a few friends.'

I didn't have any coke lying around. After my breakdown over the phantom AIDS, I was doing my best to follow doctor's orders, keeping my belt fastened and my nose clean. This meant staying home and out of trouble as often as possible.

I wasn't sober by any means, but I just couldn't afford to get high any more, in both an existential and financial sense. I was properly broke. To make ends meet I was writing shitty editorials and working in kitchens, and still I was coming up short. Every few weeks I would traipse into Cash Converters with a piece of jewellery or an appliance that a client had fenced to me back when I still sold drugs. For a $500 silver chain I'd acquired years ago, I might get $60. If I asked for more, they would shrug and tell me to try to sell it on eBay – 'Unless you don't think that's a good idea,' they would add, with a big shit-stained grin. The one thing that being wretched teaches you is that there will always be someone willing to grind you deeper into the dirt.

Even though I was broke, I had another option that night. As unfit for any responsibility as I was, due to the family connection,

I was still the contact between the house and our landlord. That meant all the other housemates paid their rent to me each week, and at the end of the month I would drive over to my aunt's house to pay her the money. Now, all that cash was just sitting there, depreciating, and I didn't see the problem with taking a little on loan.

I went to score for the Artist: I wasn't doing anything else, and the sycophant in me was excited to hang out with a semi-celebrity. Unsure how much she would need, I got about two and a half grand's worth, mostly on credit. I figured I would sell the Artist what she needed and offload the rest to friends, or snort it myself if I could find the cash. Before I saw my dealer I made a call to my buddy Doctor Paul, who I sometimes helped score in exchange for a taste, to see if he wanted anything. He asked me to save him a gram, so I had the dealer bag that up separately, and I tucked it away in my wallet.

The Artist opened the door to her house and greeted me with a warm hug, the kind where the hugger relaxes into it so they're left hanging off your neck like a stole. She was sozzled from drinking with her housemates all day and she introduced me to them in a stream-of-consciousness monologue.

'This is Liam! He's a writer! An amazing writer! You absolutely have to read everything he's ever written. Do you want a drink, Liam? You can have anything you like, as long as it's gin.'

The Artist led me to a cramped kitchen, where chairs jostled for a place at a table groaning under bottles of gin and mugs full of soft drink. She poured a fifth of a bottle into a tumbler for me, then dropped in an ice cube. We started drinking. I sold her two grams, and for the next six hours we went line for line from our bags, and talked and talked and talked about ourselves, the way only two narcissists can.

We spoke about art and love and the nebulous lines between the two and exchanged notes on how neither of us could hold down a relationship.

'My boy is perfectly fine, but he needs someone who can be his "Pizza and a DVD girl" and that's not me. I'm "The Artist".' She sighed. 'I guess sometimes you can't help but fuck up a perfect thing.'

'I know!' I grinned. 'I've followed your career.' Oh, cocaine: would this champagne existence, this sparkling repartee never end?

The Artist punched me in the arm and called me a bad word, then continued: 'An artist needs to be with another artist. We're going to feel things more fully, with greater strength than other people.' She reached out and gripped my forearm with a sweaty hand. Her eyes were full and round, like a Tim Burton character. 'Michelangelo didn't see a lump of marble, he saw a statue. Where everyone else in Florence saw a lump of rock, he saw *David* inside, and would chip away at it until he'd freed the artwork. That's what we do. I can see the shape inside the marble. That's why I like you, Liam. Because you can see inside the marble as well.'

'My God,' I said, gripping her hand, eyes filling with grateful tears. 'That's so true! Thank you!'

'Wait here! I want to give you something!' She stood up and left the room abruptly. I heard her sniffing and rummaging around in the next room, before returning with a piece of card and a sharpie. She handed it to me with a flourish, pressing it into my hands. I looked at what she'd written: *To Liam, find it in the marble*, signed with a flourish of x's and o's and a looping autograph.

I bunched up my sleeve to wipe my eyes, and my nose, which was bleeding. 'Thank you. It's beautiful.' I put it down on the table and promptly forgot that it existed.

We kept getting high until the yard outside the kitchen window was flooded with weak sunlight. I went to the toilet and when I came back the Artist was on her feet, smoking a cigarette and pacing back and forth.

'You have to go,' she told me abruptly. 'I have to get some sleep.' I was a little hurt to be turfed out so suddenly, as I was sure that I'd found my soul mate in the past sweaty hours, but I gathered up my coat and keys in a rush as she shooed me down the hallway, her hands pushing at the small of my back. I stood blinking in the chilly dawn, then drove slowly home, stopping on the way at Doctor Paul's to deliver his gram.

Doctor Paul worked a high-pressure job, spending his days and nights bringing people back to life with a defibrillator, and he had the fatalistic sense of humour that comes with that job. He liked to unwind after a long night of people dying on his trolley by snorting coke, smoking cigarettes and playing Xbox. He'd just returned from a night shift when I turned up. He welcomed me into his lounge room, where I collapsed into his couch, a capacious leather monster.

'Liam, mate,' he said, looking concerned. 'Are you all right? You look like shit.'

'I'm fine, just tired,' I slurred, opening my wallet to flip him his bag. He opened it and tapped some out onto his coffee table.

'Do you want a line?'

'I'm not sure that's a great idea.' My teeth were grinding like teenagers at a blue-light disco, and I was having trouble keeping my train of thought. 'My heart is all aflutter.'

'Relax! I'm a doctor. This is the best possible place for you to have a heart attack. I'm pretty sure it would be covered by my insurance.' He cut a couple of lines with his credit card. I smiled.

'Oh, go on then. I guess I'll get a second opinion later on.'

An hour later I was back home, taking inventory. I counted my cash and cigarettes out onto my desk, lit one of the latter and put it between my lips. I had the creeping regret that came after a night of drug abuse, that mental tally of time lost and money spent. Part of it was the suspicion that I'd shouted the Artist way too much of the coke I'd got from my dealer. I reached into my coat pocket to retrieve the bag and came up empty. It was gone. I tore off my coat and went through all my pockets with rising panic. It wasn't there. It wasn't in my jeans. It wasn't in my car. I'd lost it. Shit, shit, shit!

My mind was thick with booze and fatigue, but I could still do the sums in my head. I had the cash in my wallet that the Artist and Doctor Paul had given me, which barely even started to cover the full sum I owed. The dealer and I were friendly, but that wouldn't stop him headbutting me into a salty marmalade if I couldn't pay him back. However I ran the maths, if I couldn't find the bag, I was doomed.

I turned my room upside down with no luck. It occurred to me that perhaps I'd left it at the Artist's house. Her phone rang out once, and again. I was almost hyperventilating by this point and went through the pockets of my coat again. This time I noticed a tiny hole at the bottom of the breast pocket and my heart leaped. Using my flick-knife, I cut the lining and when the knife snagged on a seam, I tore the coat to rags with my hands. Nothing.

Still panicking, I jumped into my car and drove back to the Artist's house, so wasted I had to keep one eye closed to stop the double vision long enough to work out which tram to swerve around. I pulled up out the front of the house just as a storm broke. In jeans and a T-shirt I scurried around the kerb and alleyway that bordered the house, hoping I'd dropped the bag en route to my car. I was sweating despite the icy drizzle, and as I fell to my hands and knees to peer into a storm drain, a commuter on her way to work crossed the road to avoid me. I stared at her suspiciously, suddenly convinced that she had found my bag and was now hurrying away from me with eyes averted because she wanted to keep my gear.

A light flickered in the front room of the Artist's house. I knocked gently, then more insistently. Eventually, a sleepy-eyed housemate opened the door. I muttered something about leaving my phone behind and pushed past him into the lounge room. He went back to bed. The lounge room was empty but I could hear the shower running in the adjacent bathroom. While I waited for the Artist, I ransacked the room, checking under cushions, getting down and lifting up the corners of all the furniture to check underneath them. When the Artist came out of the shower wearing a towel, she screamed.

'Fuck! You scared the shit out of me. What are you doing here?'

I mumbled an apology and stuttered something about how I couldn't find my bag of drugs. She relaxed visibly. 'Oh no! That's awful.' She put a reassuring hand on my arm. 'I got your message and I've looked everywhere, but it's not here.' She steered me towards the door. 'If it turns up, I'll call you straight away, but right now I have to get to bed.'

She spoke firmly but gently, like a kindly schoolteacher might to a kid who'd shit his pants during sport. I mumbled more apologies and got into my car, almost weeping with frustration. I banged the steering wheel with the flat of my hand, hoping to spur my thoughts. Where was it? 'Think!' Bang! 'Think!' Bang! Then, all of a sudden, I realised where my bag was.

Doctor Paul was smiling when he answered the door.

'Liam! Mate! How are you? Everything okay?'

On the drive over, I'd rehearsed how it would go. I would settle in and gently coax a confession from Paul about how he'd nicked my bag, and he would then hand it back. If he'd already used it all, I would take cash. I would forgive him and everything would work out fine.

However, when he answered the door, grinning and high, one of the few gears still turning in my mind slipped and I pounced on him, reaching for his throat and settling for his collar. We toppled into the apartment, landing heavily on his couch.

'Oi!' he protested. 'What the fuck, Liam?'

I grabbed spastically at his head. There's a pressure point somewhere towards the back of the head where you can squeeze a nerve off and incapacitate your opponent with blinding pain, but I couldn't remember where it was just at that minute. Behind the ears? I poked at his skull while screaming, 'Where's the coke, Pauly?' until he battered me on the side of my head with his palm, which made me let go and roll off him. We both got to our feet, puffing and spluttering.

'There's your fucking coke!' Paul spat, pointing at the table. I looked over to where a few lines were ruled out with a surgeon's precision, a rolled-up $50 note next to them.

'Where's the rest of it?'

'Where do you think?'

I took that for a confession. 'Pauly, if you've taken my drugs, then I need money, two thousand, right now.'

Paul's eyes flicked across my face, taking in my twitching features, my dilated eyes, down to where the blood was pulsing through the veins in my neck. He spoke very slowly. 'Okay, Liam. You're clearly having some kind of trouble. That's okay. Do you want money?' He raised his finger to point across the room. 'My wallet is on that bench. You'll find cash inside. Take whatever you want and come back tomorrow if you need more. Okay?'

I looked at the bench, then back at him, expecting a trick, for him to rush me the second I turned my back. I edged towards the wallet, which held a handful of green and gold notes. I stuffed them all into my pocket and then flung the wallet at Paul.

'Thanks,' I said simply, and left. I closed the door behind me and stood counting the cash. It was a lot of money, but it wasn't nearly enough. I was debating whether to go back in when Paul spoke through the door.

'You're having some kind of episode, mate. You need to go home. Take a taxi and go straight home. Get some sleep and call me in the afternoon. You can have more money then. Otherwise I'm going to have to call the police, and nobody wants that.'

Back at home I fell into a deep, dreamless sleep that lasted until 10 p.m. the next night, when I woke with my head pounding and my pillow drenched in sweat and blood. I got a beer from the fridge and took stock of my situation.

In the mirror I looked like something created by a particularly untalented life-drawing student, my features warped and dented out of proportion. My skin was stretched tight over my cheekbones, but the flesh above them couched my eyes in puffy folds. One side of my head was grazed and starting to bruise an angry purple from where I'd connected with the coffee table during my scuffle with the doctor. I didn't do at all well in that fight; all my hard-earned teenaged muscle had wasted away. I was somehow emaciated and bloated at the same time, lacking both physical resources and mental agility. Dried blood caked my face from a couple of smaller cuts and an ugly red trickle dripped from my long-suffering septum. I blew my nose and the tissue came away trailing ropey strands of blood, mucus and cutting powder.

I was a paragon of health, though, next to my finances. Losing the bag had rendered me not only broke but in debt to the housemates I'd inadvertently robbed, and to my dealer, a lovely chap to be sure, but one not known for his understanding when it came to fiscal insolvency.

I considered going to confront the doctor again, but I couldn't see myself getting past security in his expensive, gated apartment complex and, besides, I didn't really want to. Paul was a gentleman, and, now that I was sober, I couldn't really believe that he'd stolen from me after all. I retraced my steps and realised my memories were staccato, punctuated by blackout jags of hours at a time. Realistically, I had to face that I was never going to see that coke again.

With the cash I had in my wallet, I could just about cover the tick or the rent, but not both. I had a little wiggle room on my credit card, but I was going to have to throw myself on the mercy of either my friends, telling them I'd lost the rent, or my dealer, hoping he'd take a kneecap as collateral.

I trudged over to my computer to check my bank account and found that it was dependably empty. I bit my lip and swore, closing the browser, which opened up the window beneath it, in which my friend Simone had sent me a Facebook message, asking how I was doing.

'Only so-so.'

'Girl trouble?'

'Something like that.'

We got to chatting and she told me how she was planning a spontaneous trip to Japan to visit a friend of hers from primary school. She was looking for flights and had found a budget airline that was offering a two-for-one deal.

'You know what would be crazy? Why don't you come? Why don't you just drop it all and come to Japan?'

I considered Simone's proposal for a while, watching the blinking green Facebook chat dot, that cheeky little will-o'-the-wisp. *Why don't you just drop it all and come to Japan?* It didn't sound crazy at all.

17

It seemed as though my time in Melbourne was up. I kept a low profile in the weeks leading up to my flight, cognisant of the fact that my
star-crossed drug baron was waiting for me in the wings. When I ran
into friends they would do double takes and look surprised, telling
me that they'd heard I'd killed myself or been murdered or left town
or something, and that they certainly hadn't expected to see me again.
Few of them lamented my absence; the city seemed to have reached
critical mass when it came to tolerating my bullshit. I'd lied to, ripped
off or cheated on nearly everyone I'd ever met, and I was finally out
of options. Most people would take me at face value, and with a

little effort I could make hunger look like passion, desperation like confidence – at least for a while. But it had all caught up with me.

The night before my flight, I was sitting quietly at a bar, avoiding my housemates, who were starting to ask awkward questions about the missing rent. A strange woman came up and tapped me on the shoulder.

'Are you Liam Pieper?'

'Yes,' I said, smiling. 'Have we met?' She smiled back, picked up my whisky and threw it in my face. 'I know all about you, you fucking dirtbag. *I know who you are.*' Then she turned on her heel and walked out.

'Thanks for reading!' I called out cheerfully, although I was thinking, *Well, that makes one of us.*

The two-for-one hadn't worked out, so I'd booked the cheapest flight on a budget airline, and it arrived in Tokyo well after midnight. Simone would meet me in uptown Tokyo in a week's time, but until then I was on my own. Standing at the airport, waiting for my backpack to roll off the conveyor belt, I listened to the burble of Japanese all around me, realised I couldn't understand a word of it, and suddenly felt immensely, overwhelmingly alone. After a fruitless attempt at getting a taxi, I took a room in a hotel next to the airport. I bought a beer from a vending machine in the hallway and used it to wash down two Valium. *Everything will seem better in the morning*, I told myself as I dozed off.

Everything did look better the next day, with the sunrise slowly warming the hotel restaurant where I lingered over a breakfast of miso and rice, a healthy, spartan meal that seemed symbolic of a new chapter in my life. I walked out to greet Japan with a gentle optimism stirring in my belly.

It was a crisp autumn morning, the sun was breaking low over the horizon, and in the distance I could see the skyscrapers of Tokyo rising from the plains. I was shivering with cold and excitement; just a few kilometres away were the bright lights, the high tech and high fashion, the weirdness, the robots and *Neon Genesis* and Miyazaki and samurai castles and beautiful women and stylish gentlemen and sushi and sake, and a million things I'd loved from afar. This was where I would start my life again.

Hoisting my backpack, I stopped on my way out the door to buy a snack from the vending machine. Something in the machine glitched and it spat out two chocolate bars instead of one. *It's an omen!* I told myself, unwrapping my lucky chocolate and heading out the door.

The bus to Tokyo was a kilometre away from the hotel gate, back towards the airport. I eschewed the courtesy shuttle in favour of walking across the sparsely scrubbed grassland and feeling the crisp air in my lungs. *It's a new day!* I thought. *Full of promise and adventure!* I went another 30 metres before I stepped on a long-dead rat hidden in the grass. It liquefied under my shoe and a murder of crows rose up from where they had been picking at its guts. The world exploded into a fury of feathers and cawing and I screeched and flailed through the miasma of angry birds, spitting distressed wails and lucky chocolate.

I boarded the bus to Tokyo and sat scraping rat off my shoe. *Never mind the omens,* I thought. *This is Japan. They have robots here.*

I was utterly smitten with Japan – its music, its cartoons, its history, its food, its sexual hang-ups, so different from and yet complementary to my own. For a month, I had the time of my life. Simone flew from Melbourne to meet me and we drank and ate our way across old Tokyo. We bluffed entrance into a musicians-only jazz bar and then when they called us up to play, I begged off with a broken arm while Simone sang.

After she went back home, I got a room in a wooden and rice-papered boarding house in the suburbs and settled down to live there for a while. If I met travellers in the common room I would tell them I was writing a novel, which I honestly planned to do but I'd yet to start it because most of the time I was stumbling drunk. Occasionally I would write a haiku about drinking, but that's as far as my work went.

My pattern for years had been to drink throughout the day, spacing it out with little bumps of coke so I could function. However, attitudes to illegal drugs in Japan are far less laissez-faire than in Australia; they attract serious penalties and the people who deal in them are serious gangsters. I couldn't score the kind of drugs I fancied without interacting with some fairly intense career-criminal yakuza types, and I was far too delicate a creature for that. When fingers start getting cut off, that's when I make polite excuses and inch towards the door.

With no access to coke or any other uppers, I just drank heavily. To borrow from my father's old Zen books or, indeed, my new home, I was all yin and no yang.

I'd start with warm sake at breakfast, then retire to my room with a couple of large cans of Asahi and fuck about with a pen and pad until it was time to go to the pub. Nights, I would sit at the bar and chat in broken English with salarymen winding down after work. They were good bar companions. The drinking culture among Japanese professionals is unique, and wonderful. When you go out with your workmates, which you are expected to often, it's perfectly acceptable to make an arse of yourself. You can slam a bunch of shots, hit on your colleagues, throw up on your shoes and take a swing at your boss, and as long as you turn up to work the next day with your tie and brief-case, nothing is made of it. The lack of ramifications appealed to me, and even if the only Japanese I knew was *'Kanpai!'*, that was enough to keep my new friends happy and buying me drinks.

After a stretch in Tokyo, I took a bus up north to Nagano, where a new friend, Fuyuki, had invited me to stay with his family, luring me with the promise of visiting a snow-monkey sanctuary nearby. Fuyuki was a professional snowboarder who'd grown up in the mountains of Nagano and spent his formative years around the buzz of the 1998 Winter Olympics. His name is written in kanji with two characters, 'Winter' and 'Tree', and there was never someone so appropriately named. He had the sparse, chill manner of a snowboarder, complemented by a soothing vagueness. You could picture him standing on a mountain, arms spread to the sky, wind whistling through his fingers, his mind empty and serene.

His English was terrible, as bad as my Japanese. We communicated via a tiny translation robot he carried with him. When he wanted to say something more complex than a few words, he would punch the sentence into the machine, which would then spit out the phrase. 'Hey, Liam,' Fuyuki would say, then turn to the machine, which would demand, 'Let's go flirt some girls.' One night when he, Simone and I were hanging out in his apartment in Tokyo, he fell asleep and started snoring. Simone and I kept talking in quiet voices until, suddenly, Fuyuki let out an earth-shattering fart. His eyes opened and darted around the room and he fumbled for his pocket translator. 'Did I,' the robot asked us, as Fuyuki looked shamefacedly at the floor, 'just rip my fart?'

Fuyuki had given me directions to his house in Hakuba Goryu in the Japanese Alps outside Nagano, instructions that looked good on paper but less solid as my bus slowly wound through a dark mountain path, snowflakes tapping on the window. I got off the bus at the stop Fuyuki had written down, to find I was standing in a pitch-black night on a nameless country road in a sparsely populated province. The driver had been reluctant to let me out, trying to communicate in mime that I would freeze to death and be eaten by bears, but I'd convinced him to open the hydraulic doors so I could step out into the blast of frigid air. As he drove off, the tail-lights disappearing around a bend in the road, I realised there were no other lights nearby. I was a long way from anywhere, and my warmest garment was the thin jumper on my back. It started to snow and I began to think that this was how I would go out, freezing to death on a Japanese mountainside. It felt foolish but somehow appropriate. I just wished I had some booze. I'd started walking with the idea of finding a vending machine with some whisky in it when Fuyuki pulled up alongside me in a BMW four-wheel drive.

As he drove me up the mountain, it dawned on me that when Fuyuki had invited me to stay 'on his mountain', it wasn't just his shitty English. Fuyuki owned the mountain. I thought I'd be sleeping on his couch, or a futon at best, but he rolled up in front of a magnificent Swiss-style chalet.

'This is your house,' Fuyuki told me through his robot. Fuyuki's mother owned a great deal of property around the mountain, including a ski resort next door. They gave me a three-bedroom chalet to crash in, winter clothes to get around in, and the keys to the BMW in case I wanted to go for a spin.

Mrs Fuyuki was a self-possessed, silver-haired lady, who that first night cooked me a dinner of *sukiyaki*, thin strips of beef that you boil and eat out of a communal pot while you get a sophisticated sake buzz on. At the table she apologised profusely that she couldn't find Australian beef at the markets, and so had settled for Kobe wagyu. After dinner, she loaned me a kimono and showed me the *onsen* on the back porch of my chalet and told me to use it whenever I felt like it. The *onsen* worked like an infinity pool powered by a natural hot spring. It bubbled up through the mountain and into the marble tub before draining off and cascading down the mountain in a steaming rivulet. Mrs Fuyuki told me to stay as long as I liked. So I did.

I spent my days hiking with Fuyuki and spent my nights in the hot tub. Every so often Fuyuki's mum would appear to offer me a cold beer, but apart from that I was alone. I stopped drinking in the daytime so I could explore the surrounding villages in Fuyuki's car without ploughing down the mountainside. It wasn't that I was averse to drink-driving – for a long time it had been my sport and pas-time – but I recognised that I wasn't used to driving in Japan, on a rocky alpine path, in a blizzard, while full of Sapporo. Soon it became too much of a chore to drive through the snow to buy alcohol, so I cut back in the evenings too. Slowly, I stopped drinking altogether.

One night I sat in the steaming water, the only light that of the moon bouncing off the mountains, and, for the first time in as long as I could remember, I relaxed. I watched as snowflakes caught by the rising steam were whipped out into the black valley below and dropped away into darkness. The whole world was still. In the perfect silence I could still hear the snow, a soft sneaky hiss as each crys-tal fell into the drifts. I was listening to that sound, warm and safe, my mind emptied out, when suddenly my conscience came barrelling back to me.

Alone on the mountain, and sober, long-dormant corners of my mind came to life, synapses sparking and creaky grey matter haul-ing long-gone memories out of storage, and I realised to my dismay that my life wasn't going so well. With nothing to dull my resurgent conscience, I was, in fact, profoundly sad.

I was also a little shocked. I'd forgotten I could feel much at all. Suddenly I found that I had a conscience and that it was as tender as a baby kangaroo out of its pouch: larval, wormlike and twitching. Trauma that I'd laughed off years ago clambered to the front of my mind and refused to be dislodged. Long-lost regrets crowded in from the back of my mind, fighting for real estate.

I could feel the guilt and anger and sadness that I'd been hanging on to for years turn up to the party, with friends. I was surprised to find that not only did I regret most of the choices I'd made since I was old enough to ride a pushbike, but that I was host to other, pedestrian remorse as well. I missed my ex-girlfriends, my cats, my friends who'd died over the years, through drugs or in cars or by their own hand. Most unnerving to me, I missed my family, the whole dope-stank, beat-down, traumatised bunch. I missed my brothers, living and dead, with the full ferocity of a clear mind. I missed my folks and their well-meaning, spectacularly misguided life advice cribbed from yoga books and Sartre. Sure, much of it was bat-shit crazy, ungrounded by God or man, and impracticable outside of a kibbutz, but it, or at least the intention behind it, nourished us as kids, and I sure could have used some of it that night on the mountain.

Psychiatrists call what happened to me the 'onset of dysphoric syndrome', alcoholics call it a 'moment of clarity', but it felt to me like the end of the party. I began to dwell on what I'd done with my life, and I was surprised that the crushing weight of years of lying to, cheating on or otherwise injuring those I'd met was still very much with me. Regrets that I'd deferred thinking through years ago rose up from the dark and found me, and each felt like trying to pass a gallstone of Catholic guilt.

It took me a few days to calm down. By the time I did, the mountain had lost its serenity. I lay awake at night, turning over the mistakes I'd made. The sensation was like coming to the end of a pointless, repetitive video game with an underwhelming ending, taking stock of wasted time and looking about the room, wondering what to do next. Most of my thoughts came back to driving down the mountain to buy a bottle of whisky, but I was scared that if I did I would neck the whole thing in the car park and end up crushed in a burning car at the bottom of a gorge, surrounded by snow monkeys hanging out for barbecue. I realised it was time to move on. My false piece of mind was shattered and in the silence my thoughts were deafening. Besides, I'd long since worn out my welcome, although if I hadn't forced myself to leave I doubt that Mrs Fuyuki would have ever thrown me out. I would probably still be there, soaking in the tub, feeling sorry for myself.

With the little money I had left I took a bullet train south to meet up with Leigh, an English backpacker I'd met while staying in Tokyo. We spent a couple of days checking out old samurai palaces in Kyoto and the endless concrete of Osaka, and then ended up in Hiroshima. There we wandered around the canals and gardens downtown like kids in a candy store, or more accurately, nerds in Japan. First we checked out a video-game arcade and spent all the cash in our pockets getting our arses kicked by children at giant-fighting-robot games. We tried to chat up some girls, then gave up and went shopping at the freakiest hentai store we could find. I found a copy of the same issue of *Bondage Fairies* the cops had confiscated all those years ago, which I bought for nostalgia's sake. Leigh came over as the clerk was ringing up the order and baulked. 'Fucking hell! If we'd known you cunts would end up this bad, we would have put some women on the ships out to that skanky little rock you live on,' he said, laughing.

Towards the end of the day we wandered onto the site of the atomic detonation and checked out the memorial museum. Sombrely, we shuffled past the photos, the piles of melted slag, an exhibition of mutant chitin that had been carved out of the bodies of children who had been exposed to the bomb. One exhibit contained the remains of a family melted into a pile of brick. I couldn't tell where the stone ended and the people began.

Afterwards we bought a bottle of whisky and sat by the river. We drank in silence, passing the bottle back and forth. I felt a little overwhelmed by everything I'd just seen and I was trying to get my head around the sheer mechanical cruelty that humankind geared itself into.

'People,' said Leigh, breaking the silence. 'What a bunch of cunts.' He passed me the bottle and we watched as a duck trailing her ducklings coasted by near where our feet were on the riverbank.

The strange thing about Hiroshima was how idyllic the whole

place was. It was a city I'd known about ever since I'd learned about the war as a child, and in my mind it was and always would be a smoking, broken metaphor. In reality, though, it was beautiful: green even in the winter, the air crisp and the streets bustling. This place that had been a radioactive wasteland not long ago was resolutely, magnificently alive.

Following this train of thought, I realised I was a little drunk, and then that I was only a *little* drunk. It occurred to me that I'd been sober for weeks, utterly bone-dry, and now I'd had a small amount to drink, and it wasn't a big deal. There was still three quarters of the bottle left, but for the first time in a decade, I didn't feel as though I had to get through it like a cat afraid of losing its dinner.

I'd gone to Japan to escape looming consequences, without any real plans beyond maybe drinking myself to death. Somewhere between landing in Tokyo and coming to Hiroshima I'd dried out. Part of the explanation was the solitude and headspace afforded by my unexpected snowy retreat, but really I'd just got away from all my bad habits long enough to find peace of mind. Or, at least, for my mind to start to piece itself together again.

So, here I was, twenty-five years old, and I was surprised to find the little devil who lived on my shoulder, and who would nudge me into action every time I heard a cork pop, was gone.

I'd blamed a lot of people in my life for my inability to stay sober – my folks, my dealers, Sensei, my girlfriends – but I'd been the instigator of just about all of my problems. I'd been waiting for some kind of inciting incident to come along and rearrange my life into something more sustainable, or even just more telegenic. Where was my dramatic low point, the one where I woke up covered in vomit and semen and shame, at the end of my tether, until Whoopi Goldberg came along to show me how to live again? Where was my rock bottom?

Rock bottom sounds like a place to have an adventure holiday, somewhere grittily exciting. The words have a connotation of resilience, of redemption, a firm surface you hit and bounce off of on the way up again. Or even a sandy bedrock a bottom-feeder like me could live off – instead of a pebbled morass of mud and shit and slime in which one could thrash about for a lifetime and do nought else. The fact was, I'd been on the bottom for ages, but I liked it there, so I didn't try to change it.

As it turns out, the way I did change, the way I stopped being a drug addict, was to, one day, after months of not even thinking about it, stop taking drugs. My time on the mountain had dried me out enough that I'd managed to gain some perspective. While I still craved drugs and booze, my body had rewired so that I didn't have to take them all the time. I'd never suspected there was a literal moral high ground, but it's right there in Nagano, three mountains over from Hakuba Village.

Just then, as I was patting myself on the back for being able to have a drink without ending up wetting myself while crying myself to sleep to a Nick Cave record, an old man walked by. As he passed, a breeze blew his kimono away from his neck, revealing a tract of burned, cancerous skin: the same weird, horn-like flesh I'd seen in the museum. I only saw it for a second, before he smoothed his robe back up, smiled politely and hurried on.

That was a moment of clarity right there: this cheerful old man walking past had had a nuclear weapon dropped on him, and I was congratulating myself on not getting blackout drunk in a memorial garden.

'You know, Leigh,' I said. 'It might be time I grew up a bit.'

'Sound. I didn't want to be rude but I was going to say that you act a bit of a fanny sometimes.'

I smiled at Leigh, passed him the bottle, shook his hand and walked off. I dropped by the inn to pick up my bag and caught a bullet train back to the Osaka airport. I was going home.

PERESTROIKA

18

It took me a while to make life work again back in Melbourne. I got an apartment on the north side of town, where I had fewer enemies, and a job working on building sites. As the weeks passed and I moved loads of brick and wood around, my shattered health started to improve and muscles started to weave themselves back along my threadbare limbs. I picked up little bits of knowledge, about load-bearing pillars, preventative demolition, retaining walls and cantilevered buildings, all of which, along with a long-forgotten degree, helped me to bluff my way into a job as a technical writer at a giant construction company.

There I realised just how much time I'd wasted pursuing crime, or, at least, pursuing the wrong kind of crime. The thing is, crime is really quite difficult. It's tense, it's dangerous, it's not as lucrative as it should be. And that was when I was a child – I hate to think what it's like these days, with GPS tracking and phones that listen in on every word. Contrary to what Sensei once told me, crime is a young man's game, and not a great game at that.

The real money, the true heist, turned out to be working for a multinational making a killing in mining and construction. I'd never even dreamed of money like that before: cash ripped raw right out of the ground with contractors tobogganing gleefully down mountains of the stuff. In a few weeks writing for the giants, I made piles of cash larger and greener than any slinging dope ever got me.

I let the chip on my shoulder about privilege fall away. I didn't need a private-school leg-up to join the resource boom that powered Australia, to be part of the national hubris. I already knew how to lie, to make one product look like another, to tuck my conscience away like a pencil behind my ear while I worked. And, just like that, I was white collar.

Once I got the cash together I paid back the money I owed all over town, and realised that I had absolutely no idea what to do next. I'd never had any plans that lasted longer than an erection, and I was at a loss as to what one was supposed to do with a lifetime.

Melbourne seemed like a strange city to me now. I walked the streets and found them at once familiar and foreign, as though some-one had built a beige replica of the town I'd grown up in. I passed by houses, hotels and shopfronts I'd partied in until I'd passed out, and I felt a twinge when I realised I would never go back there again. My mindset hadn't changed: I still wanted part of the good old days, and the stealthy caution I'd grown up using to demarcate between society and the way I lived was still there. When I saw worse-for-wear kids spilling out of a club while I drove to work, I felt a wave of nostalgia. If a police cruiser passed me on the street, my hands automatically crept to my pockets, reaching for contraband I no longer carried. Little concussions from my old life kept reaching me in my new one.

For one thing, it dawned on me that the reputation as a scoundrel I'd worked so hard to cultivate wasn't a great foundation for a life. It complicated things. I needed rehabilitation, in the truest sense of the word. I had to learn how to do everything again. Without coasting through life on a canoe of arrogance over a river of booze, I had no idea how to talk to people. I'd alienated the friends who had stuck by me over the years, and the only ones who wanted to know me now were bad news.

My relationship with my family had decayed to the point where I'd been putting in the bare minimum, and even then it was mostly to preserve the possibility of borrowing money. I'd make cameo appearances that lasted the time it took to drink a coffee, and I'd still be constantly ducking to the bathroom the entire time. Mum and Dad had grown tired of the flighty, evasive way I talked to them, when I'd refuse to answer questions about what was important to me or what I was up to because the answer to both was 'cocaine'. To anyone who didn't use, my coke-soaked arrogance was easily mistaken for garden-variety aloofness. I didn't fancy having to tell my parents that what looked to them like a serviceable life was actually a pretty thin veneer over an insatiable drug problem. For one thing, it would crush them; after Ardian's death they'd made me promise not to experiment with powders. For another, it might have incriminated Hamish, who, entering his twenties, was enjoying himself immensely, spending nights at clubs in town and daytime recovering with his friends at the family home.

My parents didn't drink, so they were kind of naive about the effects of alcohol. When Hamish was of an age to enjoy house music and its accoutrements, Mum and Dad didn't see anything strange in his coming home from a night out on the town and sitting in the backyard to drink beer for three days on end.

'Honestly, Liam,' Mum once told me wonderingly, 'they just drink and drink and drink and listen to techno. They don't ever seem to get tired. It must be all the sugar in the beer.'

So, for my good and theirs, I stayed away from the family.

The habits that had picked me up as a shy teenager put me down years later the same shy teenager, albeit one with scars and wrinkles and knuckles that ached in the winter. As a child, then throughout an adolescence that stretched well into my twenties, I'd justified my stupid adventures as experiences to be collected like points in a video game. *I could get a good story out of this*, I would tell myself as I slid into some gutter or somebody's bed. I would picture myself as an old man, sitting down and taking out his memories, polishing them to show them off, then packing them away again. Now I found myself with a fraught mind, full of booby-trapped souvenirs, rigged with anxiety, so that when I thought of a certain person, I felt a quick shock of shame, and buried it again. I'd lie awake at night, racked with guilt and doubt, old regret permeating the present with anxiety.

All the gloom I'd managed to fend off over the years found me. There was nothing to distract me from the suburban pre-fab destiny. With my first pay cheque, I saw the rest of my life augured in the neat rows of sequestered super and tax withheld; the knowledge of how many days I would spend behind a desk, the exact number of dollars I would make in a year, how much would be bled out by insurance, rent, car loan, house loan, how I would weave a cocoon of debt to grow older and sadder in.

All at once I could see the path that was laid out for me: milestones, rites of passage and the other important events I couldn't have given a flying fuck about when I was high. I saw them passing by like distance markers on the side of a highway – marriage in five years, work for next forty years, bumpy roads, divorce, estrangement from children, infirmity, the end of the line.

In the depressive wake of a wasted decade, the prospect of an ordinary life seemed terrifying beyond anything I could imagine. Sure, being held at knifepoint wouldn't be fun, but at least it'd be *exciting*. Like a hot, dusty pig, I wanted to roll in my old familiar shit. I very nearly went back to it all, and then I met someone who simply wouldn't stand my nonsense.

I met Michaela at a friend's book launch. We hit it off and made vague plans to hang out that never eventuated. I next saw her at a writers' festival, where I was trying to wrangle my one-trick pony into some kind of literary career by telling everyone who would hold still what a dangerous libertine I was. To that end, I was appearing on a panel, and I asked Michaela to come and watch. Halfway through the event I looked out into the crowd and, even though my eyes aren't great, I saw her sitting there, wearing a distinctive jumper, and got all excited that she'd come to see me. I amped up the charm as far as it would go, tried to be funny but also poignant and wise, and to project an air of world-weary sexiness for her benefit. Every time I got a laugh from the crowd I would glance at her and make mean-ingful eye contact. What I didn't know was that Michaela was there with her brother, Tim, who shares Michaela's tall, lithe build and, on this day, her jumper. After an hour of passionately eye-fucking Tim from across the room, I finished the panel and went looking for Michaela in the crowd, with no luck. I found out later that she'd left after she'd turned to Tim and told him she thought she liked me. 'Oh, no,' Tim assured her. 'He's gay.'

At a party that night I tried my hardest to convince her other-wise. We made small talk, discovered we had some friends in common and I ended up getting her phone number. I texted her the next day and we made plans to meet in a week's time when we were back in Melbourne.

The day before our date she texted me to cancel, saying she was too busy writing. Clearly this was a lie – every writer would rather do practically anything other than write – so I figured she'd just blown me off.

I left town for a few days, helping out on a film. I'd been conscripted while drunk at a party, where I'd run into a lawyer friend of mine to whom I owed a favour. He'd mentioned that his little brother, a *Dr Who* devotee, was shooting a fan-fiction film that he had written, would star in and direct. 'Actually,' my lawyer friend said, 'you would be perfect for the villain,' and I, full of wine, agreed, then forgot all about it. A few days later I received a Facebook message from the little brother, saying how pleased he was that I'd agreed to play the part.

When I got back to civilisation after the shoot up in a mountainous rainforest area, I undressed, peeled the leeches off my body, showered, and thought I'd try Michaela again. I sent her a text to ask her if she wanted to go to a movie. She said no. I was dismayed, but, more than that, perplexed. I'd never been dumped by someone before they'd got to know me, but that just made me more persistent. *Oh, I thought, a wise guy, huh?* We texted back and forth, and finally she agreed to see me.

It was the worst date ever. I'd just finished a long construction contract and I was flush with the confidence that comes with the easily won corporate dollar. I thought I could impress her by throwing some money around. I took her to a tequila bar that had an expensive menu and which I assumed would be a fun place to get drunk and get to know each other. I didn't know, though, that Michaela hated tequila, as well as fun, so things were doomed from the start.

The place was empty when we walked in, and the bar owner

brought us menus and hovered anxiously nearby while I tried my hardest to charm my date and got nothing back. Back at the writers' festival Michaela had been exuberant, articulate, funny and wry. Now she sat in stony silence and glared at me over her quesadilla. She answered monosyllabically and sighed crossly whenever I cracked a joke. Her demeanour was cold, crisp and unimpressed. She was beautiful, yes, but in the same way a glacier is beautiful as it inches down the valley to crush your village.

After an hour of trying to thaw her icy front, I wilted and gave up. She didn't like me at all. I couldn't figure out where this unrelenting hostility was coming from, but I would get the answer to that some time later.

Two weeks before, the day after Michaela and I first kissed at the writers' festival, she had been over at her friend the Artist's house for an old-fashioned girlie night, eating Japanese delivery, painting each other's nails and talking about boys.

'I've just met this guy, Liam, and I quite like him, although I suspect he's a liar. In fact, he just gave a speech at a festival about what a liar he is,' Michaela said.

At this, the Artist interrupted. 'It's not Liam Pieper, is it?' Michaela nodded, and the Artist went ballistic.

'No! No, no, no, no. Not Liam Pieper, no!'

Michaela was taken aback. 'Why, what's wrong with him?'

'He's a sociopath and a drug addict. He's just a rotten person.'

'He seems nice.'

'Do you remember when I was selling coke?'

'No?'

'Well, I did, and it's his fault.'

The Artist continued, driving her case home. 'He's such a bad person that I stole his cocaine from him, to teach him a lesson. Liam came around with some coke and when he went to the bathroom I took it, then I sold it. And I didn't even feel bad about it,' she finished. 'That's how bad a person he is.'

Michaela called a cab, cried all the way home, and didn't speak to either of us for two weeks. Then, softened by a hilarious text message from me, and the realisation that maybe a cocaine thief was just as bad as a cocaine dealer, she agreed to go out with me on a date to the tequila bar, although she was still wary that I was sitting on ill-gotten piles of drug money, which I would no doubt try to use to get her drunk and cloud her judgement.

On our date I could tell Michaela was judging me poorly, so I tried getting her drunk, buying $30 shots of rare tequilas, which she drank mirthlessly.

'Yuck.' She made a face. 'I hate tequila.'

'Do you want something else? It's my treat.'

'Why?' Michaela's eyes narrowed suspiciously.

I shrugged off what I thought was an odd question. 'Because I like you. Because I can afford it.'

'How?'

'I make a lot of money,' I said grandly. 'Honestly, you have no idea how much money I make.'

'How?'

'I work in construction.' This was true, but it didn't sound true, and Michaela glared at me witheringly. I'm slight and quite fey; I wasn't wearing a beret that night, but you could have easily imagined me wearing a beret. 'You have no idea how much they pay me.'

'Are you a drug dealer?' she demanded to know.

'No, I was once, but I got arrested and retired,' I said amiably.

Liar, thought Michaela, and then changed the subject.

After a dinner of tequila and sad, oversalted Mexican, we went to a terrible movie on Lygon Street in Carlton, then, with everything else closed, to Percy's, a dive bar across the road, where we drank bad red wine in silence. I tried to kiss her and she pushed me away. 'Yuck. Don't kiss me at Percy's.'

I was defeated. I couldn't understand what I had done to make her so furious at me. Eventually she got drunk and told me I could take her home if I didn't tell anyone about it. We went back to my house, where I asked her to wait while I ran upstairs to clean up my room, shoving dirty socks and plates and old mugs of tea under the bed, laying a new sheet over the mattress. Downstairs, Michaela, certain I was packing away a meth lab, thought about leaving but didn't.

We made out on my bed; Michaela was still hostile but resigned to her fate. 'Dinner was shit and that movie was worse,' she complained. 'The least you can do is have sex with me.' Not even that, as it turned out. Exhausted, drunk and demoralised, I collapsed, naked and impotent. Michaela sighed and rolled over, silent, then said, 'Is that a leech?'

It was a leech. The little bloodsucker was crawling up the wall. I must have missed it when cleaning up after the rainforest shoot, and it had clearly been living like a lord in my futon since.

'I guess I'll call you a cab,' I told Michaela.

'That would be nice.'

The next date wasn't as bad, and the one after that was okay, and, once I'd cleansed my room of leeches and cured my impotence, Michaela agreed to be my girlfriend. It wasn't easy, though, because for some reason she was convinced I was a tearaway and a liar. One exchange:

Me: 'Why won't you go out with me?'

Her: 'Because I'm worried you're a pathological liar.'

Me: 'I'm not a *pathological* liar. They can't help lying, which isn't me at all. Do you know what a sociopath is?'

Her: 'What?'

Me: 'Nothing. Let's go steady.'

One night, some months later at a dinner party, the group was discussing how the Artist, who by now had achieved a decent level of fame and fortune, was going. I boasted that we were friends.

'Friends?' they said. 'After she stole your coke?'

'What are you talking about?' I asked, genuinely bewildered. Across the table, Michaela flinched and changed the subject. Later that night she described what had happened all those months ago, the other side of the events that sent me fleeing to Japan, only now narrated through the prism of the Artist's perfectly self-serving world view.

After I'd heard the story from Michaela, about how the Artist had stolen my drugs so she could sell them on, I told her about the aftermath, how I'd accused Doctor Paul of robbing me, then robbed him, then fled the country, before coming back to spend months working to pay back my debts. I was cross about the money, of course, but what really boiled my potato was the Artist's long diatribes to Michaela about how she shouldn't trust me, that she would be willing to trade her friend's potential happiness to avoid making reparations for her theft.

Michaela confronted the Artist and asked her to admit to what she'd done. She just said: 'Jesus.' Michaela explained that she thought it was unfair that the Artist had robbed me, that there had been consequences, and she asked her to make amends. 'It's fine if you think he's a bad guy, but your actions would have affected other people. If you steal that much money from someone, it's going to have a ripple effect and hurt other people.'

'It's not my pond,' the Artist shrugged.

'It may not be your pond, but you still chucked a brick in it.'

The Artist shrugged again. 'Not my pond.'

Michaela started crying, came home, and cried all night. In the morning, she told me about the conversation.

'Pond!' I was flabbergasted. 'The cheek!'

'Agreed. What are you going to do?'

I didn't know what to do. Once upon a time I would have worked myself into a bluster and gone around to the Artist's house to rage and pout and get my money back, but that was a long time ago, in another life.

'It's not my pond either,' I decided.

I paid an awkward visit to Doctor Paul, apologised, and gave him back the money I'd stolen from him during my righteous psychosis. He was very good about it, said he understood and had let it go, which I was glad of. I even felt, for a second there, as the doctor shrugged and shook my hand, a strange thing it took me a while to recognise: gratitude, that stealthy fucker, had found its way into my heart. Looking back, I was struck that so many people over the years had given me the benefit of the doubt, and, while it was silly of them, I could now appreciate what it took for them to take a chance on me and to forgive me my sins, endless, recursive and vile. Most of all I was grateful for the unconditional love of my friends and family, a force undaunted by time, pure and transcendent, and surpassed only by that other kind of love, the one with blow jobs.

I'd forgotten what it was like to be in a relationship based on mutual trust. What a simple joy it was to have a confidante, someone I didn't have to lie to. I mean, I lied to Michaela plenty, but it was nice to be able to take a break sometimes, and not have to keep a running spreadsheet of my misdemeanours and felonies and whatever horse-shit I'd used to cover them up. I was in a happy relationship, but that happiness was supported by another intangibility: that somehow, improbably, life was good.

Even after everything, I had found my way back in. Perhaps, like my grandma always said, no matter how far gone I was, I had my guardians, my armies of angels and cherubim, standing over me, invisible and indefatigable, rubbing together their ethereal defibrillators, ever ready to start up my cold dead heart anew.

19

I can't point to a particular stage in my life when things got better for me. Little by little, in the tiniest increments you could imagine, I learned how to suffer minor slings and arrows without emptying my house of drugs and booze and getting caught breaking into the neighbours' house in search of a bottle of Tia Maria to send me off to sleep.

Between new friendships reminding me that people aren't born scheming and cretinous, getting sober, falling in love, and the slow drift of time, the various bruises to my heart and ego started to heal. It's not a new story, but it was a new discovery for me: how life works. You build your happiness like a bowerbird, using shiny, stolen moments to weave your peace of mind.

I had sobriety, work, a relationship. Things, in short, were good. I took up gardening as a hobby. Instead of spending my weekend swerving drunkenly across roads or trying to cauterise a knife wound with a bottle of rum and a Zippo, I pottered around my courtyard, composting and re-potting basil. I began to tune in to the seasons and rhythms of the world around me in a way I hadn't before, and wouldn't have been able to when I was floundering. Instead of dreading the cold snap that meant winter was coming and the hours I would have to spend camped out in the rain waiting on dealers, I saw an opportunity to plant garlic and beetroot. When my garden got infested, I read up on organic pest control, laying out treats to coax birds in to clear out the snails, planting marigolds and dandelions to attract ladybugs that swarmed over the aphids eating my garlic shoots, all while I stood back and laughed like a vengeful god. A vengeful, very camp god.

As part of my new life I tried to make amends to those I'd neglected and lied to along the way. I kept paying back the money I'd stolen here and there, and made apologies to the few people who would still pick up a call from me. I felt guilty about having distanced myself from my family for so long and vowed that I would do anything for them, except see them. When I did, it was under sufferance, and I was insufferable.

The problem with getting clean was that, along with sobriety, I found sanctimony. I had the born-again's zeal against sinful things, and took umbrage at the fact that my family all still really loved weed, a situation that hadn't been helped by the advent of YouTube.

In the early days of my recovery, I would use any opportunity to lord it over my family. Just like old alcoholics never really lose their mottled gin-blossom complexion, I'd absorbed some of that cocaine hubris into my being, and rarely missed a chance to turn the perfect arc-light of my sobriety onto their flaws.

'Do I want a joint, Mother?' I would sniff, adjusting my monocle. 'No, I'm rather too old for that, don't you think?'

Or, when my dad would congratulate me on landing a story in some obscure literary journal, I would hold this out as evidence that I was a superior life form. 'Well, all my success in writing, Father,' I would announce, 'is because I stopped smoking that weed. And now look at me! I'm famous on the internet!'

My behaviour was grandiose and aloof, but it was only part snobbery and rebellion against my bohemian family. It was also self-preservation. The thing is, my sobriety was and is tenuous. I still crave drugs, and have to batter down the devils when I find myself around them. Whenever I watch one of those low-rent blue-filter movies from the nineties in which some ingénue tries cocaine at the beginning and is sucking heroin out of her pimp's cock in the next reel, part of me thinks, *Oh, that looks nice*. I still drink, and although I try to keep to the glass of red wine the doctor recommends, my body doesn't want a *glass* of wine. When I have a sip, my brain sends out orders to my body to drink the rest of that bottle, and then its friends.

When I would visit my childhood home and swing open the

door to the cloyingly sweet scent of weed, it would start a disquieting craving somewhere inside me. It's not that I even liked weed, but the smell kicked off the cascade of thoughts at the back of my brain that made me wonder if I wouldn't be happier shooting goofballs somewhere in Latin America, an idea that, even now, takes considerable will to tamp down.

I developed a kind of familial holding pattern, visiting long enough to check in, but without developing any real connection to or interest in their lives. They'd long ago stopped asking questions about what I was doing or whether I was seeing anyone, and if they did question me, I dodged it out of habit. They seemed content just to know that I was still breathing, and I felt much the same way. We existed a bit like allied medieval townships built within signal-fire distance: each behind our walls, but happy that the other was still there, where we could theoretically come to each other's aid.

I didn't like visiting the home where I'd spent so many unhappy years. Spending time there brought back more bad memories than good, and it upset me to watch my little brother continuing the behaviour that I'd only recently given up myself. I couldn't help myself from growing judgemental, then angry, then sad when I popped in for a visit and found everyone propped up against ottoman stools, baked and watching Seth Rogen films. That really got to me. I raged inside my head at my parents: *Seth Rogen isn't funny! How can you find this entertaining? You are wasting your lives. It shouldn't be me giving you this lecture!* But I didn't speak up. I swallowed my frustration, made polite small talk and left.

Even though I'm a second-generation hippie, far away from my Catholic forebears, the Church runs in my veins. Long after the Catholicism has left a family, the traits run on; the tides of shame and judgement, the secrets they necessitate, they stay in the blood. Deep in each of us, the value of discretion, the clandestine church-pew whisper, the moral cowardice afforded by the Serenity Prayer. Lord give me the excuse to accept that things cannot change. Rather than make my whole stupid story a *bildungsroman* in which I head out into the wilderness, find my sobriety and bring it back home espousing the miracles of green tea like Prometheus with his flame, I just slunk away. I was sober, yes, but it made me the black sheep of the family. I went my way and they went theirs.

Then, just when I'd started to feel that they could live one way and I another, Hamish ended up in hospital.

I'd refined my visits into efficient ramraids. I would storm in, say hello, collect my mail, sit down for a cup of coffee, and maybe help myself to cuttings from the herb garden. One afternoon I'd swung past and was sitting at the kitchen table flicking through envelopes while my parents played with the cat. I asked where Hamish was and Mum and Dad exchanged a look. It was the look that children give each other when they've broken a vase and are thinking how they might glue it back together before they are busted. Finally, Dad spoke.

'We can't tell you.'

'Why not?'

'He asked us not to.'

'No?' I smirked. 'Is that so? Is he in witness protection? Has he been a deep-cover operative all these years? Is that why we all keep getting arrested?'

'He's in hospital.'

The grin dropped off my face. 'Huh?'

'He had a bit of an episode. He's in the Monash psych ward.'

'Oh . . . When did this happen?'

They did the look again.

'About a month ago.'

'A month ago!' I was dumfounded. 'And you didn't think that I might want to know this?'

'We planned to tell you when you visited. But you never come around.'

They had me there.

The psychological ward at Monash Medical Centre is down a long glass-and-steel corridor that runs off from the main entrance. To enter, you have to walk through a circuitous series of chambers where you pass anxious-looking visitors on their way in, or hollow-eyed visitors on their way out. At the end of the corridor you have to ring a buzzer, announce yourself at an intercom and enter through a heavy steel security door. I told the box who I was, then waited a few minutes before I was buzzed through.

The guy who met me at the door had a few days' worth of stubble and a gauge stretching one earlobe. His sneakers squeaked on the floor and gave a slight bounce to his gait as he came to greet me.

'Orright, mate? You must be Hamish's brother.' He had an English accent, and everything about his manner seemed designed to put you at ease. There was something of the dog whisperer about him – his body language, his handshake, all combined to present a calming front. I relaxed. He announced a visitor for Hamish and chatted as he signed me in.

'He's a good kid, your brother,' he said. 'Smart as a whip.'

Hamish met me at reception and gave me a tour of the facility. He showed me his room, which was 3 metres square with two single beds divided by a curtain. His roommate was lying in the dark and rolled over to face us when the light turned on. He was a big guy, heavily muscled and heavily tranquillised.

'Hi,' I said. 'I'm Liam.'

'Hey!' he said, and then went to sleep.

We left and closed the door. 'He seems nice,' I said.

Hamish nodded. 'He's really fun.'

'What's he in for?'

'Oh,' Hamish said mildly, 'he keeps stabbing people.'

We walked into the rec room, which had a beat-up stereo and a pool table. We played a game while he told me what had happened. It was a lengthy game, not because the story was particularly long, but because I'm shit at pool, and Hamish was medicated. We missed shot after shot, passing the cue back and forth. Every so often a friend of Hamish's would come in and say hi, and Hamish would tell me their prognosis once they left. 'This is Damien.' I shook Damien's hand. It was sticky. As he shuffled off, Hamish whispered, 'He thinks he's an angel of God – Gabriel, I think? But that's not why he's in here. He keeps trying to have sex with his mother.'

In between these social calls, a piece at a time, I got the story from Hamish.

He'd been doing a placement at a public school in a rough part of town as part of his education degree and was having a hard time with the class. The supervisor had been bullying him, and when he complained to the principal in charge of the program it got worse. So he did what our family always did in a crisis. Just like other folk might crack a beer while they sit on the couch and mull over a thorny problem, there's an old Pieper tradition of getting a little high while you try to look at an issue from all the angles. Which is fine, until you combine it with the other Pieper tradition of never letting go of a good buzz.

To deal with the stress Hamish had been smoking too many bongs and far too much meth. He lived at home, but Mum and Dad were on holiday at the time, and I, busy chasing the dollar, wasn't around to keep an eye on him as his mind started to slip. Eventually, he hit a tipping point, and, after a long bender in which he'd taken heaps of meth, coke, mushrooms and Stilnox, he was driving around aimlessly huffing nitrous oxide bulbs when he decided to die.

When he told me this I thought of a phone call he'd made to me a little over a month ago, when I'd been driving home from work, tired and cranky. He'd been high and manic, and asked my advice about suing his university.

'On what grounds?' I'd asked.

'Psychological distress,' he'd said. 'A friend of mine is being bullied and is having suicidal thoughts.' *Suicide*, I thought. *That old friend.*

'It's harder than you think suing a university. They tend to know good lawyers, on account of they make them at home. I would tell your friend to get a grip and grow the fuck up some,' I replied.

If I'd been paying enough attention to realise that Hamish's 'friend' was in fact him, I might have been more sensitive.

To end it, he took a handful of uppers, then a handful of down-ers, and then drank a bottle of vodka. It was lucky that he'd started with uppers, as the amphetamines coursing through his system stopped him from passing out before he'd vomited the downers back up.

He wasn't well though. It had been days since he'd slept, and he was having an acute psychotic episode. He was convinced he was going to die and wanted to do it at university, where they could see what they'd driven him to. He drove to the uni and tried to go to class, but they wouldn't let him in. Someone called his girlfriend, and she found him passed out on a couch in the student lounge. She took one look at him and drove him to hospital.

I put down the pool cue and stared unhappily at the wall, where a whiteboard was strung up. Someone had scrawled a Bob Marley lyric across the board. I stared at it vacantly, and realised after a moment that they'd got the lyric wrong, and had written 'None but ourselves can set you free'. *Fucking hippies,* I thought, *can't get anything right, not even hippie stuff.*

I was angry. At Hamish for taking the same cowardly way out of problems as I had my whole life; at my parents, for the example they'd set us. I was mainly angry at myself, though. Where the fuck was I when this was happening? Why wasn't I told? Why hadn't anyone called me? I'd let myself drift away from my family to the point where my little brother could end up in hospital and nobody thought to mention it to me. I was gloomy on the drive back to my parents' house, where I sat down with them to talk about what was going to happen next.

Hamish would be released in the coming weeks and would live with my folks. While we were discussing logistics, Dad got up to roll a joint.

'Dad!' I shrieked.

'What?'

'You're smoking pot?'

'Do you want one?'

I got into a flap. 'You can't keep drugs in the house. Your son is getting out of rehab. It's not fair to keep weed here. Anything could be a trigger for him. You can't let him be near drugs at all. At all.' Dad listened and nodded, in such a way that I knew meant he was going to keep stashing drugs in the house. 'You're not listening, are you?' I demanded.

'We'll keep them locked up,' Dad said mildly. I stared at him while I raged inside my head. *Why don't you get it? Why do I have to explain this to you?* Time and again I'd urged them to quit smoking pot, but it had never happened. It wasn't that they didn't try to quit. Sometimes, maybe twice a year, they would try to go cold turkey, which always made for a grim couple of days in the house. Dad could never sleep without it, and after a few days of sleep deprivation would start to fray, before losing his shit completely. Mum would overcompensate by starting to chain smoke hand-rolled cigarettes and grumpily announcing how long she'd gone without getting high. It was normally only a couple of days, and when she cracked she would keep smoking the thirty-odd cigarettes a day, but first she'd pack them full of reefer.

While Ardian was alive, when Mum was sober she'd snap at him, and he'd snap back, 'Would you just have a fucking joint, Mum?' This would offend her so much she would have to have a joint to calm down.

'You can't keep weed in the house. It's not fair to Hamish. Clean it out. Take it to a friend's house or go get high in the park like a teenager. Just get it the fuck out of the house.'

In the end, Dad did get the drugs out of the house, and when Hamish got out of hospital, the place was clean. Fresh from rehab, he continued his detox, slowly straightening out and putting his life back together. His girlfriend, a level-headed, no-nonsense young lady who doesn't take shit from suckers, has helped him to understand how things work in the world when you're sober. He has, despite everything – his own efforts to fuck it all up, my immaculate instruction in how to burn out – made it.

And as for Mum and Dad, well, a family is always a work in progress. Without the coruscating decay of a home full of pills and powders, things began to get better around the house. Mum bought a bunch of nicotine gum from the internet and went cold turkey, and she is still clean, which makes me indescribably proud.

Dad kept his weed out of the house, at least technically. Occasionally he claims to have quit, but everyone knows he keeps his stash behind the washer-dryer in the shed out back.

And, finally, after a quarter of a century, I'm starting to understand. I can't, as much as I would like to, blame my problems on my unconventional upbringing. The hippie generation passed me a torch, and I used it to burn the world down. Sure, they taught me how to think outside the law, but they didn't give me my coke problem, and they sure as all get-out didn't teach me to lie and steal and cheat. Nobody ever made me drink, smoke or snort anything except, of course, for myself, that rascal.

Many years ago, after I'd been caught hurling rocks at cars with a friend, my mum urged me not to give in to peer pressure. 'I don't care what your friends think is cool! If your friends jumped off a cliff, would you do it?' Back then I'd shaken my head mutely, but with hindsight the answer is of course, yes, I'd have been over there in a shot.

There's a lesson there that little vandal Liam could have taught me that would have saved cokehead Liam some time and money later on – which is, yes, rocks are fun, but you'd be better off not fucking around with them.

Somehow, life finds a way. My folks retired from their jobs and settled into the semi-agrarian bohemian suburban life they'd wanted for us all those years ago. They adopted another cat, an adorable Persian, who immediately started a vicious turf war with Aphrodite, our ageing, aloof housecat. The cats eat dinner with the family, off dinner plates, enjoying chicken cuts that Mum buys especially according to each cat's taste. They sit on either side of the table with their haunches on the seats and their forepaws neatly gripping the sides of the plates as they eat. Occasionally one will stop munching to look up and glare warily at the other and hiss softly before returning to the meal. I asked Mum how they came to eat at the table and she seemed surprised by the question.

'They just like to have dinner there,' she said matter-of-factly, then, more thoughtfully, 'I don't mind because they're part of the family, but occasionally it makes me worry that we might be eccentric. I don't want people to think we're nuts or anything.'

Someone once told me that a family is a group of people thrown together by fate who become weirder and weirder until nobody else can understand them. And we are, after all of it, still standing, the four of us, and our ghostly fifth. Sometimes, when we gather for dinner, I absentmindedly set a plate for Ardian, which then sits empty throughout the meal until it goes back into the cupboard, untouched. Does he, like my grandmother believes, watch over us? No matter; we watch for him.

We are all twisting kaleidoscopes, shining genetic potential that tumbles into place with turning circumstance. Hamish, more or less genetically identical to me, with similar experiences, is different. While I am lazy, he is industrious. Where I am cynical, he is hopeful; where I am vindictive, he is kind. Where I am pretentious and carnivorous in my appetites, he is more down-to-earth, living off chips and lentils. If I'd made different choices, perhaps my life would look more like his, and I'd be standing in the kitchen in Thai fisherman's pants, carefully chewing a sliver of steak to test its texture before serving, then spitting it out before it could be said to break my vegetarianism.

There aren't any hard and fast rules on how to live your life. That is what I got from my folks, and all the rest is on me.

The last time I visited we sat at the table while my mum made dinner and Dad was out 'doing the laundry'. Hamish and his girlfriend sat next to each other at the head of the table, playing footsies and whispering together. Mum set out the plates for us, and for the cats, and then went out to call Dad in to dinner. He emerged from the shed, carrying a basket of neatly folded washing, fresh, crisp and fragrant with the smell of detergent and of fabric softener and of weed, of home.

Acknowledgements

First of all, thanks to Mum and Dad who got up and went to work every day at jobs they hated to keep me fed and clothed, and still found time to read to me and teach me to dig on books. Same goes for Letitia Gregory, my first ever editor, as well as the rest of the family for inspiration. Hamish – I guess we're even for that car now.

Thanks to everyone who helped me piece together the past, a thankless, often painful game of herding cats: Carla Shallies, Avi Hanner, Nadia Toukhsati and Mel Clements, along with Vickie Shuttleworth and the National Trust.

To everyone who supported me or just made sure I didn't swallow my tongue: Jules Pascoe, Darcy McNulty, Victoria Khroundina, Dr Emma Burrows – thank you.

Thank you to everyone who read early drafts and offered notes

ACKNOWLEDGEMENTS

at all stages of writing – especially Nikola Lusk, Lorelei Vashti and Anna Krien, but most of all Sofija Stefanovic. Honestly, I don't know how anyone writes anything without you along to help. Special thanks to all the editors who threw me a bone over the years and worked to make my writing better: Kelly Chandler, Tom Doig, Zoe Dattner, Louise Swinn and Sam Cooney, and especially to Ronnie Scott, without whom nobody working in Australian letters would know shit about shit.

Thanks to all the Penguins who worked on this book, especially John Canty for designing a cover far better than the contents, Anyez Lindop, Rhian Davies and Louise Ryan for going above and beyond to persuade folk to read it, and Ben Ball for showing me that the story I'd originally had in mind was only the tip of the iceberg, and also that I had to put more effort into my metaphors. Extra special thanks to Bridget Maidment for delousing the final draft.

And, of course, to Cate Blake. I've heard it said that authors who lavish praise upon their editors are victims of Stockholm syndrome, but I have been in worse hostage situations before. Thank you, Cate, for carving the still-beating heart out of my truly awful first drafts, and for making me remove all the literary references and song lyrics.

And the most gratitude for the great green light of my life, my Michaela; God only knows what I'd be without you.